GRAŻYNA BACEWICZ

Women in Music

Series Editors

Anna Beer
Oxford University
Alyn Shipton
Royal Academy of Music, London

This book series creates a platform for ground-breaking studies which offer new insight into any and all aspects of women in music. Building on Equinox Publishing's established lists in popular music, film music, and the wider industry, the series is of interest to the scholar, practitioner, and general reader.

Women in Music aims to be inclusive, seeking to publish historical and critical studies, cultural analyses, life-writing, traditional musicology and more. The series as a whole works to challenge some of the less helpful divisions in music scholarship – for example, between 'popular' and 'classical' – by welcoming submissions which range, where appropriate, across genres, eras, and disciplines. The common thread, however, remains women's lived experience, whether as individuals or groups, and/or cultural understandings of the category of 'woman'.

Almost all areas of the music industry are now waking up to women's under-representation, and not just as a historical phenomenon. Change nevertheless remains slow. Through the dissemination of the latest scholarship in the field, *Women in Music* not only celebrates and explores the often hidden contributions of specific individuals and groups, but by contributing to a richer, more complex, picture of women in music, provokes some important questions for the industry.

Published

Dora Bright: Her Life and Works in the Public Eye
Anthony Bilton

Hired Guns: Portraits of Women in Alternative Music
Amanda Kramer and Wayne Byrne

Grażyna Bacewicz

Joanna Sendłak
Translated by Halina Maria Boniszewska

SHEFFIELD UK   BRISTOL CT

Published by Equinox Publishing Ltd

UK: Office 415, The Workstation, 15 Paternoster Row, Sheffield, South Yorkshire, S1 2BX
USA: ISD, 70 Enterprise Drive, Bristol, CT 06010

www.equinoxpub.com

First published in Polish as *Bacewicz* by Joanna Sendłak, published by Polskie Wydawnictwo Muzyczne 2022. This first English edition published by Equinox Publishing Ltd 2024.

© 2022 by Polskie Wydawnictwo Muzyczne, Kraków Poland. All rights reserved. This English translation © Halina Maria Boniszewska 2024.

 This publication has been supported by the © Poland Translation Program.

All rights reserved. No part of this publication may be reproduced or transmitted in any form or by any means, electronic or mechanical, including photocopying, recording or any information storage or retrieval system, without prior permission in writing from the publishers.

British Library Cataloguing-in-Publication Data

A catalogue record for this book is available from the British Library.

ISBN-13 978 1 80050 504 9 (hardback)
         978 1 80050 505 6 (ePDF)
         978 1 80050 609 1 (ePub)

Library of Congress Cataloging-in-Publication Data
Names: Sendłak, Joanna, 1966- author. | Boniszewska, Halina Maria, translator.
Title: Grażyna Bacewicz / Joanna Sendłak ; translated by Halina Maria Boniszewska.
Other titles: Bacewicz. English
Description: First English edition. | Bristol, CT : Equinox Publishing Ltd, 2024. | Series: Women in music | Includes bibliographical references and index. | Summary: "Grażyna Bacewicz (1909-1969) was a composer with an individual, expressive style. She was also an excellent violinist, a very fine pianist, and a talented author. This biographical story, based in large measure on letters and other family documents, has been brought to us first hand by the composer's grand-daughter, the writer Joanna Sendłak"-- Provided by publisher.
Identifiers: LCCN 2024022321 (print) | LCCN 2024022322 (ebook) | ISBN 9781800505049 (hardback) | ISBN 9781800505056 (pdf) | ISBN 9781800506091 (epub)
Subjects: LCSH: Bacewicz, Grażyna. | Composers--Poland--Biography. | LCGFT: Biographies.
Classification: LCC ML410.B08 S4613 2024 (print) | LCC ML410.B08 (ebook) | DDC 780.92 [B]--dc23/eng/20240514
LC record available at https://lccn.loc.gov/2024022321
LC ebook record available at https://lccn.loc.gov/2024022322

Typeset by S.J.I. Services, New Delhi, India

Contents

	Series Editor's Preface Alyn Shipton	vi
1	Early Life: Łódź	1
2	Student Days: Warsaw and Paris	18
3	Marriage and Recognition	26
4	War and Resistance	36
5	Compositions between Performances	52
6	Art versus Realism	59
7	Achievements and Losses	71
8	Distant Travels and Family Matters	82
9	A Final Creative Outpouring	100
	Chronology of Life and Work	113
	Selected Works	120
	References	123
	Further Reading	125
	Index of Names	126

Series Editor's Preface

One of the principal aims of the Equinox series *Women in Music* is to shed new light on significant female musicians. As will become apparent from just the first few pages of Joanna Sendłak's biography, her grandmother Grażyna Bacewicz was remarkable in a significant number of respects. A gifted performer from childhood as both a violinist and pianist, she also began writing music from an early age. And, despite the disruption of two world wars, she flourished as a composer and performer for the rest of her life, with an extraordinarily prolific work-rate. Furthermore, she did not stand still, but continued to develop, exploring sonorism and serialism, and consistently producing new work that was true to her own principles of creativity. She maintained this, even when the political climate in Eastern Europe after World War II sought to impose a restrictive aesthetic framework on composers.

She was also a gifted writer, producing a number of semi-autobiographical short stories, as well as numerous letters to her extended family that not only reflect on her creative process, but (because her musical life allowed her to travel outside Poland and escape state censorship) give a very candid account of what life was like during and after the Stalinist era. There have been other biographies of Bacewicz, but this book is exceptional in that Sendłak had unfettered access to family papers, and inside knowledge of her relatives, that allowed her also to explain the biographical elements in Bacewicz's fiction. It is a privilege to be able to add her candid writing to the Equinox list.

I would like to thank all at Polskie Wydawnictwo Muzyczne, and in particular Marta Turnau for making this edition possible, and to the Book Institute Poland Translation Program for their support. Finally, I'd like to express my gratitude to the translator, Halina Maria Boniszewska, for bringing the book to our attention, her sensitive work in creating the English text, and catching the mix between formal and informal expression that is such a hallmark of Joanna Sendłak's writing. I very much hope that one result of this book's detailed account of Grażyna Bacewicz's life is that new listeners will discover her music, and come to appreciate a performer and composer whose musical achievement on every level was remarkable. Whether writing chamber music, such as her *Piano Sonata No. 2*, or her *String Quartet No. 3*, or working with orchestral forces as in her *Concerto for String Orchestra*, her music has gained and maintained its place on the international stage. Hopefully this book will help to shine light on several of her other distinguished, but less well-known, compositions, and bring them to new audiences.

Alyn Shipton
Royal Academy of Music, London
Series Co-Editor, *Women in Music*

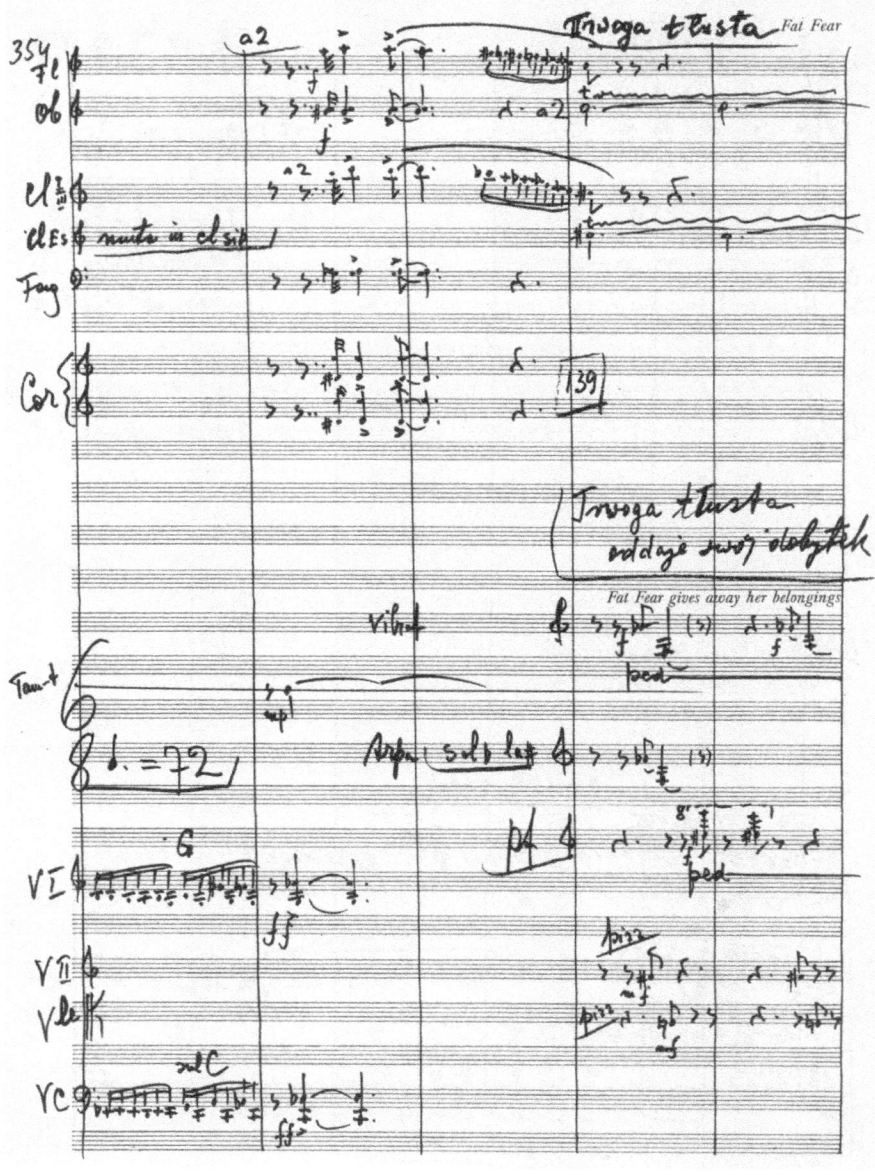

Excerpt from Grażyna Bacewicz's final work, the ballet Desire (1969)

1 Early Life: Łódź

Maria and Vincas meet

Grażyna Bacewicz's life began in Łódź. The third child of a mixed marriage, she was born to a Polish mother, Maria Modlińska, and a Lithuanian father, Vincas Bacevičius. We discover where and when Grażyna's parents met from Maria's reminiscences in her private diary from the 1950s. In September 1953, visiting her beloved Łódź for the first time since 1945, the sight of familiar places triggered memories: 'After breakfast, we walked around Łódź, where in 1898 I had met and fallen very much in love with my husband. We got engaged on 19 May 1901, and until our wedding on 28 June 1903, we both worked, my husband in education, while I worked in a bank and then in a pharmaceutical warehouse, in the accounts department. We were very happy.'[1]

We do not know the circumstances in which Maria and Vincas met. They were both possessed by a passion for music, so it is possible that they became acquainted at a concert organized by one of the factory owners in Łódź. It is likely that during the five years of their acquaintance, they often went to concerts. Perhaps they attended the Łódź Music Society, whose president at the time was Henryk Grohman. At some point, they may have attended a piano recital by Aleksander Michałowski, which seems likely, given the fact that as a young woman, Maria's mother had taken piano lessons with Michałowski himself. It is worth noting that at the time, music lovers in Łódź had the opportunity to listen to excellent pianists, including Józef Śliwiński and Moriz Rosenthal.

We can only imagine Maria and Vincas's first meeting. There they were in the concert hall: she, a petite, elegantly-dressed blonde, fizzing with energy. When she noticed the strapping Lithuanian in the doorway with his fashionably-clipped moustache, his mass of blond hair, a well-cut (though not new) suit, she glanced at him with interest. For his part, instead of listening to the music, he gazed at her for so long that she became flustered and lowered her eyes. After the concert, Vincas went up to Maria and bowed.

'Are you a pianist?' he asked.

Maria lifted her head and smiled. 'I'm afraid not, though I'm not too bad at playing the piano. I work in a bank. How about you?'

'I teach music. I play a bit of violin. I believe that music allows children to develop harmoniously. I couldn't live without music!' he assured her, earnestly.

'You know, my mother, Natalia Zdzitowiecka, studied with Noskowski and Michałowski. She could sight-read the most difficult pieces beautifully. She used to give charity concerts. My father also played, and he was even inclined to composition. At home we were forever playing on the harmonium and assorted pianos.'

'Really? Are you at all interested in the theory of music?'

'I'm mad about it,' Maria assured him, letting him take her gently by the arm. They went out into the street.

'I'm sure you play the piano splendidly…' Vincas awkwardly resumed the conversation.

'All the children at home took lessons with Mrs Wieczorkowska. (I remember it perfectly.) There were these little pouffes she would place under our short legs to stop them dangling,' said Maria, laughing.

Vincas coughed in embarrassment. He realized that this beautiful woman came from a high-class background, while he was born in the Lithuanian countryside, though into what was admittedly an educated, land-owning family.

'Do you live in Łódź?' he asked, to change the subject.

'I'm staying with family, along with my sister Aniela. We've suffered a terrible loss; our parents died quite suddenly, and they were so young as well…'

'I'm so sorry to hear that; it must be so hard for you,' Vincas sighed, and he gave her arm a compassionate squeeze.

'My name's Maria, Maria Modlińska,' she introduced herself, smiling, taking his hand in her warm fingers. 'Are you well acquainted with the city?'

'I've just arrived. I'm going to try and get a post at the Aleksander Zimmer School. I've been studying music theory and singing, but I'd also like to teach general and theoretical subjects. That would increase my prospects on the labour market.'

'You absolutely must sing something for me!'

'That would be an honour for me. Can I see you again?'

'Why, of course! Maybe we can play something together? I adore music, and I've really missed it since my darling mummy passed away. The silence at home is terribly depressing.'

Vincas made a low bow, as if she were the queen.

Maria said goodbye to him outside her grandmother's house. She ran quickly up the stairs, to tell her sister all about the handsome Lithuanian, fascinated by the extraordinary inner strength that emanated from him.

Maria the idealist

Following a request from her then grown-up son, Vytautas, Maria Modlińska wrote down many details about her family history in a letter to him. She was born in Warsaw on 8 April 1871, one of five children, to an engineer, Stanisław Modliński and his wife Natalia (née Zdzitowiecka). Maria's father was related to the Dąmbski family, nobles who owned many properties in central Poland, including in the counties of Opoczno, Łowicz, and Kielce. Stanisław's brother, Józef Modliński, had properties in Jasieniec and Braki in Łowicz county, where Maria presumably spent many a holiday. The Modliński coat-of-arms was the Tępa Podkowa – a golden horseshoe against a sky-blue background, its toe end uppermost, with a cross in the centre, a helmet above, and topped by a crown with an eagle's feather emerging from it. Stanisław had a responsible role as one of the 'senior engineers of the city of Warsaw'.

Maria's mother came from the village of Zdzitów by the River Horyn.* Maria's grandmother was the daughter of the court doctor to King Stanisław August, while her uncle, Władysław Zdzitowiecki 'emigrated to France after the January Uprising of 1863** in his capacity as emissary to the Princes Czartoryski and Radziwiłł. Frequent trips to Rome enabled him to reach the rank of Chamberlain in the court of Pope Leo III and earn the titles of Chevalier of the Tomb of Saint Gregory, Commander, and Count'.[2]

Maria received a good education. In her youth she attended the Marian Institute for Young Women of Noble Birth and, following the sudden and premature death of her parents, took courses in administration and economics and obtained a post at the Warsaw branch of the Petersburg Bank. For a while she worked in Trzech Krzyży Square, opposite St Alexander's Church, but as her grandmother on her father's side lived in Łódź, and as she and her younger sister, Aniela, were in Warsaw on their own, she found work at the Łódź branch of the firm Ludwik Spiess and Son.

Maria was an idealist, and did not attach importance to a person's origins so much as to their inner worth. What mattered was how well they did their work – this was a value that her mother, a concert pianist, had instilled in her. Whatever really happened at Maria and Vincas's first meeting, their mutual feelings turned out to be unusually strong, leading Maria to marry a man who would be considered beneath her, in terms of the social norms of the day. She said 'Yes' to her beloved 'Vincuk' (as she called her husband many years later in the diary that she kept until her death).

---

*   Translator's note: Currently within Belarus.
**   Translator's note: In 1863 Poland was under Russian occupation. The 1863 January Uprising broke out in protest against forced recruitment of Polish youth into the Imperial Russian Army. It lasted from January 1863 to autumn 1864 and ended in defeat for the Poles, with further repressions and executions and tens of thousands of Poles being forcibly sent to Siberia.

Like Vincas, Maria had a strong and independent nature. Perhaps it was the loss of her parents or the need to move to another city that helped her find the determination to disregard material discomfort, to follow her heart and marry the humble music teacher from the Lithuanian region. In doing so, she gave up the comforts of the old world and threw herself energetically into the whirl of her new life. In her view, the world was racing towards modernity, and her mind was preoccupied with positivistic challenges. Towards the end of her life, she wrote about this in a letter to her son, Vytautas: 'My husband and I worked hard, without any help, from early in the morning till late at night, which was never enough time, as there was so much work to be done. Nowadays, when I take my mind back to more than half a century ago, to my childhood years, I see that in our family home, we effectively had more servants (nursemaids, butlers, and a cook) to help us than we had people in the household. I also see how everyone in our family, each in their own profession, now works from dawn till dusk, and the household, and a large one at that, runs without any help. With this whirl of work, the crazy technological progress, and the pace of work in every field, everything from the olden days seems to me to be some kind of unreal, peculiar, funny dream, and I wouldn't go back to those times. I may be old, but I love working, and I want to continue to be active until the day I die and witness the crazy progress of this world.'[2]

Vincas the stubborn

We need to remember that Vincas Bacevičius arrived in Łódź in late 1898 or early 1899, but before that occurred, he spent a long six years moving further and further away from his home territory, which was the Lithuanian village of Muraszkowizna (from 1918 known as Ardzijauskai), a small settlement hidden among thick forests in the Marijampolė district. The village fell within the Wysoka Ruda (Višako Ruda) parish and, at the time, had twenty-two people living in it. Vincas, a son to Piotr and Anna (née Aliszewska), was born on 16 May 1875. By the age of 18, he was independent-minded and stubborn, though a very courteous person, who loved music above all else. In 1893, while at the Veiveriai Teachers' Seminary, he passed his teacher training examination, and then he started looking for a post. As it turned out, finding work was not so easy, particularly for Vincas, who supported the idea of national revival for Lithuania, so as a 'disloyal, subversive element', along with the majority of the teaching profession, he was banned by the Czarist authorities from teaching in Lithuania.*

---

* Translator's note: Between 1795 and 1918, Lithuania was ruled by Imperial Russia.

What could he do? He wandered into the depths of Poland. There, he worked in a number of different village schools, drawing inexorably closer to Łódź. He worked in Restarzew (Łask county), Szarlej (Częstochowa county), Stobiecko Szlacheckie (Radomsko county), Leonów (Piotrków county), and Czyżemin (Łódź county), until he finally reached Łódź. It was there that in 1898 he met Maria Modlińska.

On a freezing-cold day, 15 January 1899, Vincas arrived on the doorstep of a private music school in the city. He shook the snow off his worn-out coat, took a deep breath, and headed straight for the head-teacher's office. After a long conversation with the head, Aleksander Zimmer, during which Vincas presented an uncompromising stance on music's superiority above all other art forms, and after demonstrating his musical skills (and he was a good violinist who had been a member of the school orchestra in Veiveriai), he was offered a post. Vincas worked there for a few months, possibly until the end of the school year, which then made it easier for him to find his dream job in a different private music school. Fortunately, there was a growing demand for professional music teachers, as schools were just beginning to offer not just singing lessons, but lessons on different kinds of instruments. Orchestras were also being set up, while the inhabitants of Łódź were fast turning into sophisticated music lovers.

From 1900 to 1901 Vincas taught at Józef Majer's School; from 1901 to 1906 he taught at Kazimierz Hessen vel Goetzen's School. It was during this time (in 1903) that he married Maria Modlińska, thereafter having a family to support.

After arriving in Łódź, Vincas continued with his professional development. Whenever he had any free time, he would study music. He was now able to play not only the violin, but also the piano; and he sang as well. In 1899 he had begun studying at the Hanicki Brothers' School. The school closed three years later, in 1902, but the stubborn and ambitious Vincas continued to take private lessons with his former teachers. He took a course in music theory with Alojzy Dworzaczek, and he refined his solo singing skills with Antonina Korwin-Kossakowska. Through the efforts of some of its old students, the former Hanicki Brothers' School was transformed step by step into two institutions, both of which offered teaching qualifications in music. Later, in 1911, one of these became the Helena Kijeńska School, and it was this school that Vincas and Maria's future children would attend.

The young married couple

The Bacewiczes got married in Warsaw on 28 June 1903. The ceremony took place in the baroque Church of the Lord's Transfiguration, known as the Capuchin Church, on Miodowa Street. After the wedding, the couple settled in Łódź. It is quite possible that in December 1903, when Zygmunt Noskowski gave a lecture there on rhythm in music and compositional form (as part of a series of lectures organized by Antoni Grudzieński, a former teacher at the Hanicki Brothers' School), the newly-weds would have been in attendance. Their mutual passion for music made up for the modest circumstances in which they would be living for the next few years. Vincas had few possessions at the time. He owned a violin, a few books, a lamp, a table, a bed, some basic pots and pans, and two changes of clothing, which we learn from his application for financial aid from the school authorities. As a music teacher, early in his career, Vincas had frequent changes of employment. In 1906, by which time he was a father to two sons, Vincas found work at the school within the Karol Scheibler factory complex, where he spent the next eleven years working as a singing teacher. This employment gave him the regular income that he needed to support his growing family. He left this post at the age of 42, when the school reduced its size and its teaching staff. This took place at the end of the school year 1916–1917.

In September 1917, Vincas then took up a new post at School Number 32, a smaller Polish city school at 84 Przejazd Street (now Tuwima Street), where his new head-teacher was Antoni Tomaszewski. At that stage, his firstborn son, Kiejstut, was 13 years old; Vytautas 12; Grażyna 8; and his younger daughter, Wanda, barely 6.

One can well imagine what sort of conditions the Bacewiczes created for their children, given that three of them went on to become professional musicians. (The exception was Wanda – a born poet.) It seems that the secret of the family's strength came from their love of music, as well as the need to create, which was accompanied by a constant effort at spiritual development. As a father, Vincas worked very hard, and so he had high expectations of his children, instilling in them the need for self-improvement. All of them, without exception, became art enthusiasts who believed in the beauty and harmony that was also manifest throughout the entire universe. Their home was filled with music. Mr and Mrs Bacewicz's little children, like those in Maria Modlińska's family home, 'took music lessons with little pouffe stools placed next to the piano, to stop their short little legs from dangling'.

'Without any little nails…'

The Bacewiczes initially settled down on Widzewska Street. They later moved to one of the workers' houses that had been built in the late nineteenth century by Karol Scheibler, a factory owner from Łódź. These ran in straight terraces along the northern side of Wodny Rynek Market Square and beyond, by the cotton mill on Księży Młyn, along Świętej Emilii Street (now Tymienieckiego Street) and Prządzalniana Street. From 1875 onwards, where these roads intersected, stood Księży Młyn, the mansion where Scheibler's daughter, Matylda, lived with her husband, Edward Herbst. The brick cotton mill, monumental in size, towered above the road. It was surrounded by rows of massive commercial buildings: a dye-works, a finishing shop, and four warehouses. The workers' houses stood in three rows, with six semi-detached buildings in every row. Their brick walls, identical staircases and windows heightened the impression of the insignificance of the individual human being, caught up in the cogwheels of modern technology.

Over a period of ten years, the family moved house several times. On the first occasion they moved their meagre possessions from Widzewska Street to Fabryczna Street; then they moved to 67 Przędzalnia Street; in October 1918 they were given a place at 15 Księży Młyn Street, in a school building at No.1 Factory School, where Vincas taught; they eventually moved to 8 Szkolna Street (now Mielczarska Street).

While Maria might have been planning to give birth to their first son in Łódź, things turned out differently. The place of birth entered in Kiejstut Bacewicz's birth certificate is the village of Muraszkowizna in Lithuania. Many years later on 12 June 1952, Maria wrote in her diary: '13 VI 1904, at 4 in the morning, our first little Son was born, following a difficult and dangerous struggle both on his part and his mater's, since this Little Boy of Ours was intent on glimpsing God's World upside down with the Lithuanians.'[1]

This short entry in the 81-year-old Maria's diary, in which she rarely revealed her emotions, suggests that Vincas, who badly wanted his first son to be born in his own country (and whose birth certificate does indeed have him recorded as a native-born Lithuanian) probably deliberately set off for his homeland with his pregnant wife. Luck was on their side, and everything turned out well. Many years later, in 1986, in response to a question on the dual national identity of the Bacewicz siblings, Kiejstut replied as follows: 'How did this Polish-Lithuanian home life of ours look like on the inside? It's true to say that when the four of us were children and of school age, our daily life took place under the influence of the Polish cultural tradition, and we all spoke Polish at home and attended Polish schools. But it's also true to say that, alongside the Polish, the Lithuanian national element was also present within our home, and it must have played a part in forming our minds. Our father was a living embodiment of this, and of the Lithuanian cultural tradition. Our father's parental influence, along with our visits to his family home in Lithuania, gave us close emotional ties to that country too. So, both within our consciousness and imagination, alongside the Polish thread, the Lithuanian thread was always alive.'[3]

On 9 September 1905, the Bacewicz family welcomed a new son, Vytautas (affectionately called Witek), into the world. But apart from the birth of his son, the year brought Vincas a painful loss with the death of his father, Piotr. Piotr was buried in the cemetery in Wysoka Ruda, and years later, a mature oak shaded his grave. It had been planted there by his two sons, Vincas and Petras. On that day, Maria had stood and watched as the brothers had dug a hole and placed the sapling in it. She had heard the scraping of spades as they struck rock, and the splashing of water being poured from an enamel watering can onto the sapling.

On 5 February 1909, a third child was born to Maria: a long-awaited daughter, Grażyna. On her daughter's 43rd birthday, 5 February 1952, Maria wrote in her notebook: 'Grażyna was born during the daytime, at around 3 p.m., without any little nails on her fingers and toes, as she was born at seven months. For some time, I kept this little Angel wrapped up in cotton wool, and I wept, as my darling Vincuk had been expecting a third son, but he later came to love this tiny little daughter so very dearly as well.'[1]

'Have you two gone mad?'

No doubt, even as an infant, Grażyna would have been subconsciously picking up soundwaves from the music played in the home. This is how, many years later, she described their childhood in her short story, '*I Wstęp – liryczny*' ('Prelude I – lyrical'), the opening chapter in her memoir collection *Znak szczególny* (*A Distinguishing Mark*): 'I slept in a cradle, my brothers in little beds (my sister hadn't yet been born), surrounded by sounds coming from a cello, a violin, a piano, sometimes a human voice, or even a trumpet. (Now that we know it's possible to learn in one's sleep, it is understandable that all three of us became musicians.)

'But a crotchety relative of my parents did not approve of the situation: "Have you two gone mad? Clearly, you want your children to end up in a madhouse!"

'My father would ignore this elderly lady. She would then have a go at my mother:

'"For mercy's sake, don't you realize that when children are in a deep sleep, they need to have peace? Can't he just stop ('he' meaning my father) tiring the boys out during the daytime? Anyway, whoever heard of teaching such little ones to play on two instruments?"

'My mother wasn't bothered about these warnings.

'The elderly lady wouldn't back down with her "mission". She would catch them unawares, call in during the evenings, always unexpectedly, checking to see if they were paying heed to her advice. She eventually took offence. She may as well have been talking to a brick wall, for all the effect her words were having. She abandoned her evening invasions, and she also stopped coming round during the daytime. In fact, she never showed up again. Peace returned. And then we "poor little sleeping ones" were finally able to listen uninterrupted to the sounds of our future.'[4]

The Bacewicz's youngest daughter, Wanda, was born on 10 August 1911, the only one of their children to be given a Polish name. Like her siblings, she graduated from music school, but her professional career revolved around literature, journalism, and poetry in particular. When she was a little girl, young 'Wandzia' loved listening to the music that her brothers and sister played; nevertheless, she avoided practising herself. Grażyna recalled that period in her short story: '*II Wstęp – jeszcze bardziej liryczny*' ('Prelude II – even more lyrical'): 'I'm now five years old. I'm catching up with the boys – especially with my violin-playing. It's not going so well on the piano. My younger brother, Witek, is unsurpassable. In any case, rivalry wouldn't even cross our minds.

'We already have a trio. My father, a maximalist, would prefer a quartet. He has started "bothering" the youngest of us, Wanda. Prematurely, I think. Even a teacher with a good reputation at the school where he works, can behave in a pedagogically inappropriate way at home. He is impatient. He longs for a quartet. Wanda longs to read poetry. She hides under the table. She thinks no-one will find her there. She isn't yet four, but she gets totally absorbed in her reading.

'My brothers are now "young bachelors" – each with his own distinct personality. Kiejstut – a philosopher, focused, maybe even secretive. Witek – eccentric, dashing, full of unexpected ideas. Wanda – well, she does play, but without any enthusiasm. She is always disappearing under the table. There is only I who, when they tell me to practise, I practise; when they tell me to play scales, I play scales. But it's boring. I should have rebelled.'[4]

During the children's early years, they were home-schooled by Vincas. He taught them general subjects and gave them all musical tuition on two instruments – violin and piano. The children had lots of tasks to do each day, as that was what their father expected of them. From the apartment adjacent to the school where Vincas taught, one could hear the muted singing of the choir that he conducted. In the afternoons, as she darned the children's clothes (which were passed down from older sibling to younger sibling), Maria would listen to the scales and finger exercises that were persistently practised by her children throughout the changing seasons and which, without warning, could change into harmonic-sounding complicated phrases. From the windows of the 'famuła', as the two-storeyed brick workers' houses that formed part of the residential area of the Scheibler factory were called, Maria would look out onto the grey street, to see what the weather was like. Sometimes, when Vincas was paid his teacher's wages, she would treat the children, to slightly soften the rigours of their study-focused way of life. She would take them to the factory shop, known as the 'konsum' and let each of them choose their favourite sweets – chocolates in coloured wrappers, or transparent jellies that smelled of raspberry. The children would gobble up their goodies so quickly that they never managed to bring any back home with them.

The siblings cherished these special moments as they walked along by the low red-brick houses that ran on forever. They would pass by the Herbst Palace and stop not far from the pond. The corner of Przędzalniana Street and św. Emilii Street was where two worlds met. When they stood looking at the Księży Młyn (Priests' Mill) residence, they could imagine the villa's elegant interior. Similarly rich quarters were also located in the Scheibler Palace that stood near Wodny Rynek (Water Square; now Victory Square), which had been rebuilt by the Warsaw architect, Edward Lilpop. The walls of the study, the mirror room, the dining room, and the Moor's room were lined with patterned wallpaper, panelling, imitation gilt leather, murals, and even mosaics (dated 1886) by the Venetian glass manufacturer Antonio Salviati. When the taste of the sweets turned into nothing more than a memory, they would return home. On their way back, they would pass emaciated workers who were barely able to stand up after their daylong shift at the factory. They would open the creaking door that led to the staircase and take the rear entry out into a tiny yard, with a brick wall running all around it. This was their playground. In the springtime, the tiny violets that grew on this little patch of earth would remind the children that in the summer they would be getting their freedom back again, that they would be running about in the wild Lithuanian meadows and, in the evenings, hearing the wolves coming out to the edge of the forests. Or they might be visiting their mother's family in the Kielce region, or one of the noble manor houses in the Górno countryside, where they would be obliged to follow certain norms and conventions, and instead of galloping bareback, the girls would have to ride their horses ladies' style, side-saddle, struggling to keep their balance.

They regularly spent their holidays in Lithuania at their father's family home, right up until the outbreak of World War I in 1914.

A thinking, rational woman, Maria Modlińska believed in a logical, orderly, and therefore deterministic reality. She tried to pass on that kind of vision of the world to her children. She believed in the purpose and rationality of the civilization that was developing before her very eyes, in constant positivistic progress.

Years later, Kiejstut commented: 'We owe it to both our parents for having brought us up to revere science, art, and creative work, and for having passed on their human values to us in general. In short, we had, in the form of our parents, quite exceptional guides – open-minded, open-hearted people who, in addition, possessed great strength of character. It was our father [...] who taught each of us to play on two instruments from early childhood – piano and violin (he also taught me to play the cello), as well as the basics of music theory, and he cultivated in us the discipline of collective music-making, forming chamber ensembles at home. Consequently, he gave us brilliant training for our later studies at the Helena Kijeńska-Dobkiewiczowa Music Conservatoire in Łódź. Not only that, but he also prepared us for public performance from childhood onwards.'[3]

'A chair for *Mademoiselle* Grażynka!'

To mark the end of the school year on 25 June 1916, Factory School Number 1, at the Scheibler complex where Vincas Bacevičius taught, organized a musical evening for pupils and parents in Braun's Garden. At number 64 (now number 68) Przędzalniana Street, there was a workers' club, which had been built in 1884–1885 and extended further in 1894. It contained a library, a reading room, a restaurant, and a dance hall called 'Braun's Hall', as well as the garden. The highlight of the concert, as seen on a poster from the time (which also lists choral performances and reading recitals by individual pupils from the school) was the musical performances by three members of the Bacewicz family from Łódź: seven-year-old Grażyna, twelve-year-old Kiejstut (written 'Keistutis'), and ten-year-old Vytautas. The proceeds from the concert went to support the boys and girls at the school who came from low-income families.

One can well imagine that in the spring of 1916, as she busied herself around the home, Maria must have noticed that the music her children were playing was beginning to sound better and better. The boys were tackling Beethoven's cello and piano sonatas numbers 2 and 4 (in C major and G minor respectively) with real passion. In the afternoons, their father would take Vytautas to school and sit him down at his piano. On one of these occasions, as he was playing, the door swung open.

'My dear colleague: would you be so kind as to tell me what your son is playing?' the headmaster's voice boomed out across the room.

'His own composition: *Fantasy on War Themes*,' Vincas said proudly.

'I hear your daughter's not half bad at playing the violin?'

'Yes, Grażynka, though she's only seven years old. But Kiejstut is in his second year at Helena Kijeńska's.'

'Then maybe they could all take part in the end-of-year concert? You could decide on the programme and who's to perform. What do you say to that?'

'It would be an honour, Sir,' Vincas assured him, and the headmaster struck his cane on the floor in approval.

From that day onwards, Maria became enveloped by waves of sound. The boys practised their Beethoven and played Chopin's *Polonaise in G flat major* as a piano duet. Vytautas, in addition to his own composition, played the *Fantasy* from Bellini's opera *The Sleepwalker* on the piano and worked at Harold J. Henry's *Cavatina* on the violin. Kiejstut, meanwhile, in addition to the duet with his brother, practised *Awakening of the Lion* by Anton de Kontski. Little Grażynaka practised Émile Pessard's *Andalouse*, Opus 20, number 8 in piano arrangement, while on the violin she worked at Mozart's *Minuet* and Benjamin Godard's *Berceuse* from his opera *Jocelyn*.

Maria made them some elegant clothes, and on the day of the concert she took great care over styling Grażyna's auburn locks. Then they set off for Braun's Garden. It was a good thing that the headmaster had saved them some seats, as the entrance to the garden was crowded with parents who had yet to buy their tickets, though they could have done so during the week had they popped into the Gebethner and Wolff bookshop on Piotrkowska Street.* A seated ticket cost thirty kopecks. Minimum entry cost ten kopecks. Maria sat down in the front row, fixed the green bow in her youngest daughter's hair, and the two of them listened with great attention to the performance by the school choir. Grażynka was third to go up on stage. She walked up energetically, curtsied, sat down at the piano and began to play. Her little legs swung in time to the music, as if she were dancing. When she finished her performance, the audience clapped for a long time. A moment later, she reappeared on stage carrying a tiny violin: a quarter-size, child's one.

'Please may we have a chair for *Mademoiselle* Grażynka,' the amused headmaster signalled to the caretaker.

People began murmuring as the caretaker went up on stage, picked up the little girl, and stood her on a chair. And when the last note of the Mozart piece was heard, the audience went absolutely wild. There was no end to the uproar. Grażynka had performed in public for the first time in her life.

Throughout the concert that evening, the Bacewicz siblings were either passing each other on the steps up to the stage or meeting up on stage to perform the next piece. Vincas watched them nervously, his brow furrowed, while Maria thought back to her childhood, to her mother, Natalia Zdzitowiecka's concerts. She felt proud once again, and was overcome by a warm feeling.

After the performance, all four children went on holiday to their relatives in the Lithuanian countryside. When they returned to school in 1916, Kiejstut went into his third year of study at the Helena Kijeńska Music School (which changed its name the following year to become the Music High School). He concurrently attended the Józef Piłsudski Specialist Maths and Science High School (known today as High School III on Sienkiewicz Street), where he studied mainstream subjects. He grew up to be a serious boy who looked at life from a philosophical distance. Vytautas had crazy ideas and developed an interest in occultism. The girls, by contrast, particularly Wanda, were interested in the humanities and loved literature. In 1919, Grażyna began attending the Janina Pryssewiczówna Private Girls' Humanities High School on Sienkiewicza Street. A year later, Wanda followed in her footsteps. Like her brothers, Grażyna also attended the Music High School. After a year studying piano with Helena Kijeńska, Grażyna was admitted to a higher-level course. She had violin lessons with Feliks Wiesenberg and Feliks Dzierżanowski. She

---

*   Series Editor's note: Łódź was the site of a major World War I battle in late 1914 between Russian and German forces, but after the Russians withdrew, the city with its population of half a million people was under German Imperial control from 6 December 1914 until the end of the war in 1918. It was sufficiently far away from the subsequent fighting, which was focused mainly in Silesia and the Carpathians, to remain relatively peaceful, and social events such as this concert were able to take place.

studied harmony and counterpoint with Jan Maklakiewicz and harmonic analysis, organology, and aesthetics with Szymon Waljewski.

When the youngest of the siblings, Wanda, finally joined her brothers and sister at music school, Vincas's secret dream was fulfilled. All four of his children were now studying music at an advanced level, and what was more important, music had become their passion, which might, in the future, lead each to a life as a professional musician, maybe even a composer. In Vincas's opinion, only a creative occupation could guarantee a fully-rewarding existence, as artists are naturally able to distance themselves spiritually from the ever-changing circumstances of life over which no-one, after all, has any control.

Over the 'green border'

The economic crisis that beset industrial post-war Łódź made it impossible to provide for four children, let alone their music studies.* In the reborn Poland of the 1920s, industrial centres were rocked to their foundations. The Bacewicz family struggled daily with ever-increasing financial difficulties. To supplement the family budget, Kiejstut, Vytautas, and Grażyna took part-time jobs, often playing in the cinemas and theatres of Łódź, as silent film pianists.

Vincas decided to find a post in Lithuania. Ever since the end of World War I, when an independent Lithuanian state came into being, he had frequently thought of returning to his native land. The year 1923, however, turned out to be a bad time for a return of this kind. The continuing dispute over Vilnius aggravated the mutual distrust between the Poles and the Lithuanians. The Poles were in favour of reviving the union or having a federation, while the Lithuanians were keen on asserting their national identity.

After many a sleepless night and much deliberation, the family agreed that once he had found work in Kaunas, Vincas would regularly send home a specific amount of money to support the family, and would later bring the family over to join him. In Maria's opinion, Vincas's decision was a desperate one. Years later in her notebook she recalled that they had, after all, jointly brought up 'four children and had, together, sweated away tirelessly until the year 1923, when in July the tragic moment arrived that was to separate the family forever'.[1]

Vincas, a Lithuanian who by this time had been residing in Poland for many years, asked the authorities for permission to leave, but was met with refusal. This is how Kiejstut described the event: 'When, in 1923, the authorities made

---

* Series Editor's note: Following the end of World War I, the huge textile industry in Łódź was stymied in one direction by a German/Polish customs dispute, which effectively reduced exports to the west to a trickle, and in the other by the Russian revolution, which ended profitable exports to the east.

it difficult for my father to leave for Lithuania, not wanting to give him the required permission, and even going as far as blackmail by offering to grant him permission to leave without the right of re-entry, he decided to take a radical step. He entered Lithuania illegally over the green border, taking the decision to remain in his country permanently and take an active part in the creative efforts of his nation.'[3]

Maria felt in the depths of her soul that she would never see her husband again. Nevertheless, thanks to his work in Kaunas, the family was able to survive these most difficult years. He began by sending home the equivalent at the time of twenty dollars, so that a year later Kiejstut was able to start his studies in philosophy at the University of Warsaw.

Vytautas was the first of the siblings to visit his father in Kaunas in 1926. He spent a year studying in the humanities department at the University of Kaunas. Later, wanting to get to know the world and to widen his horizons, he left for Paris to further his academic career. He spent several years there, studying music and attending philosophy lectures at the Sorbonne. Vincas, meanwhile, spent 1927 working as a teacher in the Aušra Boys' Secondary School in Kaunas, where he taught music and directed the school choir and wind orchestra. When in 1931 Kiejstut arrived in Kaunas with his young wife, Halszka, his father passed on his position to him, in this way showing how very much it mattered to him that his children worked to support Lithuanian culture. He secretly dreamed that his son and daughter-in-law would settle permanently in Kaunas.

Theme and Variations

But let us go back to the year 1921. In the autumn of that year, a new teacher arrived at the Helena Kijeńska High School: Kazimierz Sikorski. He taught music theory, solfeggio, harmony, the rudiments of music, counterpoint, musical form, and history of music. On matters musical, Professor Sikorski saw eye-to-eye with his young student Grażyna Bacewicz. Many years later, he recalled that she was a child with outstanding musical ability, possessed of an excellent ear and memory, and, most importantly, was exceptionally hard-working. It was then that Grażyna, aged 12, started composing, influenced perhaps by the composition classes that she was taking with Sikorski. She destroyed many of her early compositions, as she considered them insufficiently good. She was already a perfectionist. The earliest of her works that she kept was *Theme and Variations*, which she wrote when she was 15 years old; in other words, three years after she first started composing. As a mature 55-year-old, Grażyna Bacewicz recalled her schooldays as follows: 'In those days I attended the Conservatoire for harmony and counterpoint. I wasn't obliged to produce any compositions, so to speak. My attempts were spontaneous and voluntary. I neither knew how to, nor wanted to, defend them. From those first attempts,

I already knew that my ambition, my main aim in life, was going to be to write music.'[5]

During the 1920s, the Helena Kijeńska High School underwent significant development. In 1922 it changed its name to the Helena Kijeńska Music Conservatoire in Łódź. Another new member of staff appeared at the school to take up the position of piano teacher. He was a graduate of the Saint Petersburg Conservatoire and a private pupil of Teodor Leszetycki. We are talking about Kiev-born Antoni Dobkiewicz, who later became Helena Kijeńska's husband. He also became the teenage Grażynka's piano teacher.

It might have been Antoni Dobkiewicz to whom Grażyna showed her earliest piece (the one she considered worth keeping), the afore-mentioned *Theme and Variations*. One can well imagine how: 'On a certain day in the summer of 1924, just before the end of the school year, with a holiday-like atmosphere in the air, Grażyna Bacewicz opened her school bag, took out a sheet of paper, covered with tiny handwriting, and placed it on the piano music-stand.

'"I wrote this recently," she said and began playing energetically, her slim, unusually long fingers running across the keyboard. She had no trouble stretching to a tenth and playing the kind of intricate chords that no-one else could play.

'After she had finished, her teacher went up to the piano stand, picked up the sheet of paper and scrutinized it so closely that his nose practically touched the paper. He stared at it intently, and the moment stretched itself out so much so in Grażyna's mind that she practically got lost in the space between the sound and the word.

'"Did you write this yourself?" her teacher eventually asked her, looking searchingly at the fifteen-year-old girl, whose round face bore more resemblance to a nestling's than a fledgling's.

'The young girl nodded her head and took the sheet of paper back off him, as if she were afraid that her teacher's short-sighted eyes might erase the notes from it.

'"It's brilliant; it's interesting, very inventive. Interesting figuration, ornamentation, varied textures, changes of key. And a short fugato, where you repeat the main motif in the key of E major: very interesting. Are you familiar with Szymanowski's *Variations* in B flat minor, opus 3?"

'"No."

'"You must listen to them; you have something in common. Thank you for showing me your piece, Grażynko; it's an honour for me. I think I'm going to propose to the Teaching Council that we have a performance of your composition at next year's concert at the Conservatoire."'[6]

As promised by her teacher, Grażyna did indeed get to perform her composition. She first set foot on the stage of a philharmonic concert hall on 7 June 1925. This was during the annual concert by conservatoire students, which was held at the Łódź Philharmonic. Here she gave the premiere of her *Theme and Variations*. At a similar concert in 1927 she performed Mendelssohn's *Piano Concerto in G Minor* with orchestra. A short time later, on 26 February 1928, also on the stage of the Łódź Philharmonic, she gave the first performance of *Two Preludes and Fugues*, which she had composed in 1927. Apart from her own compositions, she also played Nikolai Medtner's *Sonata in D Minor* and the *March* from Sergei Prokofiev's French-language opera, *L'amour des trois oranges* (*The Love for Three Oranges*).

Reviews of the concert in the Łódź press described Grażyna Bacewicz as clearly inclined towards the most recent, newest directions in music and displaying a great virtuosic temperament.

Professor Kazimierz Sikorski, who had awakened in Grażyna her passion for composition, did not stay long at the school in Łódź; he left for Paris in 1925. He was replaced by Kazimierz Wiłkomirski, a cellist and an excellent teacher who, years later, wrote in his memoirs: 'I taught Bacewicz counterpoint, introducing her to the intricacies of fugal construction, clarifying in detail the rules for creating a real answer and a tonal answer. I can recall that the written exercises of this exceptional (and not at all "easy") pupil contained numerous departures from the strict rules that I had previously given her, against which this future composer rebelled constantly. "Does it necessarily have to be like that? Why? Why can't it be done differently?" In answer to those kinds of questions, I would usually reply that it was to do with the unshakeable logic of a musical idea, being the essential element of a fugue as such. But Grażyna wasn't easy to persuade.'[7]

From Łódź to Warsaw

Grażyna worked away energetically on further compositions. She was already writing polyphonic music. The forms and techniques she used were the result of her rational considerations as a composer, and she was restrained in how she arranged her musical material.

During her school years, in addition to the *Two Preludes and Fugues* already mentioned, she also wrote *Three Fugues* for piano, *Song* for violin and piano (which also exists in a version for voice and piano, set to the composer's own text), *Two Double Fugues* for string quartet, as well as a *Double Fugue* for mixed *a cappella* choir. She was undoubtedly more absorbed in all this composing than she was in her studies for the leaving exam at the Janina Pryssewiczówna High School. No-one in her immediate circle had any doubt what her choice of further study would be. Encouraged by her mother and her older brother, Grażyna planned to leave for Warsaw. She dreamed of attending the State Music Conservatoire. This seemed a feasible step, as Kiejstut had already moved to Warsaw (in 1924) and had taken a teaching diploma in piano at the Conservatoire. At the same time, he had been studying philosophy at the University of Warsaw where he had been exempted from paying tuition fees. He had taken these studies so exceptionally seriously that, for a while, the family had been concerned that he might abandon music for philosophy.

In July 1928, when Grażyna took her school-leaving exam and completed her studies at the music conservatoire in Łódź, the family also had a special celebration: at St Alexander's Church in Warsaw, Kiejstut Bacewicz married Halszka Baranowicz, who was still studying voice at Warsaw Conservatoire. The marriage lasted for the rest of their lives: the next 65 years.

Maria had to make an important decision. Following discussion, both with her children and (by letter) with her dear 'Vincuk', she decided to leave Łódź and, with her daughters, return to Warsaw. This was not an easy decision. The family needed Wanda to finish her music studies at the conservatoire first and pass her leaving exam at the Janina Pryssewiczówna High School, following her sister's example.

We may imagine the family weighing up all the pros and cons relating to the move after the wedding reception, which Halszka had organized at their rented flat at 2 Dobra Street in Warsaw.

'But Mummy,' said Kiejstut, attempting to put an end to the discussion, 'please don't worry; Grażynka can live with us, can't she?'

'But wouldn't I be a nuisance to you?' Grażyna was concerned.

'On the contrary. My dear little sister, Halszka will be pleased to have your company, as I'm out of the house all day at my philosophy lectures, or else sitting in the university library.'

Halszka, who was still studying voice with Adela Comte-Wilgocka, nodded her head to show that she agreed with her newly-wed husband.

'We'll go to our classes at the Conservatoire together!'

'But I'd also like to hear some philosophy lectures; it sounds awfully interesting,' Grażyna put in.

'You see, Mum; in my opinion, a little bit of independence will be good for a young lady of nineteen,' Kiejstut summed up in a reassuring tone of voice.

So it was decided. After the summer vacation, Grażyna went off to Warsaw to study music. Meanwhile, their mother and Wanda made gradual preparations for their move out of Łódź. When a year later, the two of them arrived in the capital and took up rented accommodation on Długa Street, Grażyna welcomed their arrival with relief. With her innate delicacy, not wanting to hamper the young married couple any longer with her presence, after a few months of living with her brother and sister-in-law in their flat, Grażyna had taken a sublet of a room on Dobra Street in the city. Unfortunately, this had not been the best of solutions, as she had difficulty tolerating the presence of strangers on the other side of the wall, particularly while composing. In her opinion, a composer's work demanded full concentration, absolute privacy, and peace and quiet.

2 Student Days: Warsaw and Paris

Hurrying off to the Philosophy Department

The academic year 1928 turned out to be the beginning of a new, independent life for Grażyna. With her characteristic enthusiasm and energy, she set to work. By curious coincidence, her composition teacher at the Warsaw Conservatoire turned out to be her former teacher, Kazimierz Sikorski, who had returned from Paris. In addition to composition with Sikorski, Grażyna also chose two other subjects: violin with Józef Jarzębski and piano with Józef Turczyński. As if that weren't enough, following Kiejstut's example, Grażyna also signed up at the Philosophy Department of the University of Warsaw, where she joined other students at first year lectures. She attended Professor Władysław Tatarkiewicz on ancient and medieval philosophy, Professor Henryk Elzenberg on 'an introduction to the philosophy of values', and (of course) lectures on the 'psychology of the emotions and the will', which were given by Professor Władysław Witwicki. Lectures on the history of philosophy in Poland were given by Dr Wiktor Wąsik, while those on 'philosophical definitions' were given by Professor Jan Łukasiewicz. In addition to all this, Grażyna also took a course in the Lithuanian language. The following year she took Japanese lessons with a Buddhist Doctor of Theology, Ryōchū Umeda. It was Kiejstut, with his fascination for the culture of the Far East, who persuaded not only Grażyna to attend these courses, but Halszka and her sister too.

It is not difficult to imagine how full the young student's timetable was, or the eagerness with which she would run from the Conservatoire to Krakowskie Przedmieście Street to lecture hall number 9 on the first floor, where she would seat herself behind one of the dark wooden benches and listen to lectures where ethical and aesthetic problems were being considered. She was going to be able to discuss her thoughts not only with Kiejstut, but also with someone who was attending lectures at the Sorbonne: her other brother, Vytautas.

However, after her first year of studies, Grażyna understood that this excess of courses was taking her away from what she most wanted to do: composition. During her second year, she continued to attend philosophy lectures, but she did not take any exams in the subject. She was highly selective with her choice of courses. Ultimately she wanted to devote her time solely to music, particularly to what she regarded as her most important subjects. She began concentrating solely on composition and violin. Her pianistic skills were already at a professional level, which enabled her to perform her own compositions for piano.

In her short story '*Skandal*' ('Scandal') of the 1950s, Grażyna describes a performance of her own compositions. Having been asked to play a piece on piano, she overhears a stage whisper from a shocked member of the audience, who asks the person sitting next to her: 'Since when has she been playing the piano?'

These words are overheard by a certain well-known wit, Tadeusz Marek, who never misses an opportunity to have a bit of fun. He leans over, so the lady can better hear him, and whispers: 'Miss Bacewicz learned to play the piano yesterday – just in case.'[4]

'Szymanowski – yes; his music – no'

During the time that Grażyna was a student at the Conservatoire, the institution was going through a crisis. The school-like structure of the place was evolving into one that reflected an institution of higher education. In 1927 Karol Szymanowski was appointed director, and in 1930 he was made rector. He introduced several reforms during his tenure as director. However, as Kazimierz Sikorski recalled many years later, a group of conservative-minded teachers, led by Piotr Rytel, Eugeniusz Morawski, and Stanisław Kazuro, overthrew the reforms in 1931: 'Szymanowski resigned; the teachers that he had appointed were kicked out. Me included. This was just as Grażyna was about to take her diploma… My students were harassed, as in many cases they had left other professors for me; [students] like Szałowski, for example, Palester and Panufnik, who had started off with Rytel… Grażyna was also harassed in 1932 for having been in my class. She took her diploma exam before a panel chaired by Rector Morawski. They gave her a 'four' grade. She laughed about that four grade later. She understood perfectly well what was going on.'[8]

A maverick, Grażyna went her own way throughout her student years. This was not a period conducive to innovative creativity. She tried not to be influenced either by neoromanticism or by Szymanowski's music. The student community used to say: 'Szymanowski – yes; his music – no', thus asserting their reluctance to emulate his style of composition.

In January 1929, Grażyna composed a sonata for violin and piano, a clear step in searching for her own sound. And although in the first two movements, her style does on occasion approach Szymanowski's, the third movement – an agile, witty, lively one – already shows the beginnings of her future language as a composer. Six months later, she wrote her *Sinfonietta* for string orchestra, which she submitted for her diploma exam in 1932, along with a violin sonata (probably a sonata for solo violin, also written in 1929) and a *String Quartet* written in 1931 (one of two that she had composed at that time). It is not unfeasible that the harsh criticism from her examiners contributed to her decision, shortly afterwards, to withdraw both quartets from her official catalogue of works. For her diploma, she also composed the Psalm setting *De profundis clamavi ad te, Domine* for solo voices, choir, and orchestra, as well as a few small pieces. The sole piece to have survived out of all those that Grażyna composed for her exam is *Psalm CXXX* [*De profundis...*].

'A young star has appeared'

In April 1930, two years before she took her diploma exam, Grażyna visited her father in Lithuania. She gave a violin performance in the hall of Kaunas Conservatoire, where she played pieces by Handel and Grieg, as well as her own sonata for violin and piano.

Sprawled out on a chair, her father grunted with satisfaction as he read a review. 'My dear little daughter; they're calling you a young star that has appeared in Lithuania.'

Vytautas coughed and added: 'They've described you as a first-rate violinist. They're saying that you deserve to be seen as one of the best violinists! Listen to this, everyone: "Bacewicz's interpretation is outstanding for the excellence of her technique, a truly feminine delicacy, an expressive temperament, and a clear intonation – the characteristic features of a virtuosic interpretation."'[8]

'You don't need to worry about anything; after your diploma, come over to us, to Kaunas,' Vincas called out in delight.

'But, Dad; I'd like to go and study in Paris, like Vytautas.'

'Maybe we'll manage to get you a travel scholarship, or maybe they'll give you a position in the orchestra here. Who knows?' said her father, dreamily.

'But Paris...' Grażyna sighed.

'We'll write an application to the Lithuanian Ministry of Culture for a scholarship for you,' her father added.

As he accompanied Grażyna to the railway station, he handed her a letter to his beloved wife, Maria. 'Give that to your mother and do whatever you can to persuade Wandzia to come and visit me; I miss her,' he said, as he waved good-bye to his daughter.

'She's a girl, but she plays the violin…'

Prior to being given a 'four' grade in her final exam in composition, Grażyna passed her violin diploma with honours. Stefan Kisielewski, who was a fellow student at the time, was in the audience, listening attentively. This is how he later described his impressions: 'She played with energy and gusto, very clearly and precisely… In fact, her slight figure, her focused energy, a kind of passionate ferocity towards the music were extremely evocative and demanding of respect. I was personally hugely impressed that not only did this girl play the violin, but she composed as well. "What kind of a born musical demon is this?" I thought to myself.'[9]

At the end of her time at the Warsaw Conservatoire, Grażyna had fun sending up some of the professors (in a subtle way, naturally, with a light note of irony) when she composed *Three Caricatures* for orchestra. In these she portrayed her teachers: Józef Jarzębski, Grzegorz Fitelberg and Kazimierz Sikorski.

Before her second trip to Lithuania, she wrote in a letter to Vytautas: 'Should the *Caricatures* end up in Kačinskas's hands, do write and tell him that in this piece I have consciously used the instruments to humorous effect. We also need to add a short programme note (just a few words) about the *Three Caricatures*, that *I* is a comic representation of a violin lesson with Prof. J.J. [Józef Jarzębski]; that *Car. II* is the conductor F.G. [Fitelberg Gregorz], who enters with pomp, does a bit of flirting and then goes back out with more pomp; and that *Caric. III* is dry Prof. K.S. [Kazimierz Sikorski]. So it's a dry fugue.'[2]

As is usually the case, between the writing and the performing of the pieces, quite a bit of time elapsed. The first performance of *Three Caricatures* was given by the Polish Radio Symphony Orchestra in 1933, with Grzegorz Fitelberg conducting. In later years, the conductor regularly performed Grażyna's new compositions.

Before these compositions were heard in performance, both sisters went to Lithuania together to visit their father. Kiejstut and his wife were already there, in Kaunas. Kiejstut had been awarded his longed-for master's degree in philosophy on 24 February, 1931. For his final examination, he had submitted a dissertation to the exam board with the title: *An Analysis of Hume's Views on Goodness*. He had also passed a whole series of difficult exams in the history of ancient and medieval philosophy; in logic and general methodology with basic concepts in mathematical logic and key themes in the theory of knowledge; in general psychology; in the history of modern philosophy; in Polish philology; and in ethics and the psychology of ethics.

In Kaunas, Kiejstut had taken over his father's position at the secondary school, while Halszka had signed up for voice lessons at Kaunas Conservatoire, with Professor Władysława Grigaitiene.

Vytautas, meanwhile, had been putting great energy into developing artistic activity within Lithuania, even producing a monthly publication, *Muzika ir Teatras*, for which Kiejstut began writing articles on music on his arrival in the country. Grażyna often performed at concerts with Vytautas. Amongst other places, they also appeared at the theatre concert hall in Kaunas, where Grażyna performed Szymanowski's *Źródło Aretuzy*, some Spanish pieces, and her own *Caprice No. 1* for violin and piano. They also travelled to Riga. Critics noted that in her *Caprice*, the young composer showed an excellent command of the expressionist style. They also praised her expressive playing, which was devoid of any romantic sentimentality.

From Vincas Bacevičius's point of view, everything was working out for the best. His children were now beginning to make a real name for themselves within Lithuanian artistic circles. Unfortunately, however, Grażyna was unable to find work in Lithuania, either in an orchestra or at a music school. Her applications were constantly being turned down. Eventually her father suggested that she apply to the Ministry for a scholarship to study music in Paris. If this plan succeeded, any problems with finding work would sort themselves out, as all scholarship holders, on their return, were obliged to take up positions in Lithuania.

Unfortunately, Grażyna's application for a scholarship was turned down. Years later, in a letter from 1966, referring to the events of that time, Vytautas reminded his sister: 'Grażynko…and then I took you to Paris. That was a turning point in your life, though it was a very painful one at the time for our Father, who, being a logical man, straightaway admitted that you were right, which he often later wrote about in the letters he sent me to Paris.'[2]

Vincas's dream that his daughter identify with his beloved homeland ultimately evaporated. One day in 1932, he accompanied his daughter to the station where she was catching the train to Paris. They embraced warmly, then Grażyna jumped into the carriage. As the train started moving, letting off clouds of steam, she began to wave; she waved and waved for a long time, not stopping until her father's diminishing figure disappeared into the distance.

Rue Lamandé first time around

Interwar Paris, brimming with freedom, noisy with artistic novelties, embraced creative artists, among whom there was a large group of young Polish composers.

Grażyna stayed in a house full of Polish musicians on Rue Lamandé. She signed up for advanced studies in violin (with André Touret) and composition (with Nadia Boulanger) at the École Normale de Musique. She became a member of the Association of Young Polish Musicians in Paris. Her friendship with Nadia Boulanger would last for years. Much later, in 1974, in a filmed interview, Professor Boulanger said: 'I don't think that we teachers can give our students more than they already possess. Bacewicz's talent had been formed in Warsaw by Sikorski, whom I had the pleasure of meeting and whom I admire. Grażyna, like nearly all my Polish students, arrived with a solid musical education: both classical and modern.'[10]

Grażyna Bacewicz's first stay in Paris lasted less than a year. During that time, she composed six pieces, including *Witraż* (*Stained Glass Window*) for violin and piano, *Convoi de joie* for orchestra (which had its premiere in Warsaw in 1934 with Grzegorz Fitelberg conducting), *Children's Suite* for piano, and her *Wind Quintet*. In May 1933, she entered her *Wind Quintet* for a competition organized by the Société Aide aux femmes de professions libérales (Society for the Aid of Women in Liberal Professions). She won first prize (*ex aequo*). She was awarded a certificate and 1000 francs in prize money, which she used to repay her brother, Vytautas, at least in part, for the financial help he had given her, which had enabled her to pursue her studies in Paris.

At that time she frequently performed at concerts run by the Association of Young Polish Musicians in Paris. She even travelled to Nice for a concert co-organized by the association Amies de Musique de Chambre (Friends of Chamber Music). After that, she and her friends carried on to Majorca. Grażyna described the journey in her short story '*Gdzie jest twoja ciocia?*' ('Where is Your Aunt?'): 'I dreamt of palm trees, of the southern natural world of Africa. Admittedly, Majorca isn't Africa, but finding myself halfway between Europe and Africa was also alluring.

'Four of us went: Łabuński (composer), Hennertowa (singer), me (violinist), and Sulikowski (pianist and accompanist). We took the opportunity to visit Barcelona, as that was where our ship set sail.'[4]

(Her African dream came true much later on, after World War II.)

Bacewicz shared a cabin on the ship with a few elderly Spanish ladies. Following lengthy questioning, the venerable old maids had to acknowledge the fact that the young Polish woman was travelling around Europe without 'her mother, her aunt or a guardian'.[4]

Composer's concert and Paris again

On her return from her first stay in Paris, Grażyna threw herself into a whirl of concerts. This time, when she played in Lithuania, it was Kiejstut who accompanied her. Their performances were given favourable reviews. In January 1934 in Vilnius, Vytautas conducted his sister's *Three Caricatures*. It might have been due to the publicity generated by these good reviews that only two years after her graduation, the Warsaw Conservatoire put on a concert of Grażyna's works on 10 May 1934. The programme was a very rich one indeed. The composer decided to perform two caprices (which she later withdrew from her catalogue of works), *Witraż* (*Stained Glass Window*), *Andante and Allegro*,

Lithuanian Song, Theme and Variations for violin and piano; and her piano pieces: *Sonatina No. 1* (also later withdrawn), *Children's Suite*, and *Scherzo*. She also planned a performance of her *Quintet* for string instruments (which had been awarded the prize in Paris). Grażyna donated the entire proceeds of the concert to the students' mutual aid organization, Bratnia Pomoc (Brotherly Help).

Had we found ourselves in the audience at that time, we would have been able to see the slim figure of Grażyna communicating wordlessly with the pianist Jerzy Lefeld (whose page-turner was the 21-year-old student, Witold Lutosławski). She might well have talked with her accompanist after the concert, and on being asked what her concert plans were, might have admitted that she would like to try her hand at the Henryk Wieniawski Violin Competition, which would be taking place in Warsaw in 1935.

'Grażynko, apparently the brilliant Carl Flesch is popping over to Paris.'

'It would be marvellous to get a bit of guidance from him.'

'Take a few lessons with the master,' Jerzy suggested, as he put his sheet music back into his big, leather satchel.

'Why not? Maybe I'll go to Paris before the end of the year,' she murmured. In her mind's eye, she could see the charming little backstreets of the city she loved. She did not wait long to put her idea into action.

A jinxed competition

In her memoir, *Pech (Bad Luck)*, Grażyna recalled her lessons with Carl Flesch and what she went through during the Wieniawski Competition: 'I did some solid preparation – under Flesch. I worked with him for six months. He used to really tire me out, and he sometimes even got angry with me, but he did wish me good luck when I left. (It's a pity that I didn't knock on unpainted wood at the time.)

'The competition had two rounds – the standard very high... I got through the first round successfully, and playing a difficult programme at that, including Bach's *Prelude and Fugue in C Major*.

'Afterwards, our musicians ran up to me, looking very pleased indeed. I heard them whispering: "Well, we've already got one prize..."

'At the time I was living with my mother and my sister, Wanda, on Długa Street. All three of us were following the competition, so, obviously we weren't at home in the apartment in the evenings.

'The second round was easy; we had to play two movements from one of Wieniawski's concertos – with orchestra, of course.

'Nearly all the competitors, including me, chose the *Concerto in D Minor* (the one in *F Sharp Minor* – which, in my opinion, is not as good – we only heard about twice, if I remember rightly).

'The day before my performance, we were sitting calmly in the Philharmonic. In the intervals, I flirted with Dr Andrej Biernacki – my future husband. He walked us home and said good-bye at the gate. We had to wait an unusually long time for it to open. When we eventually found ourselves in front of the door to our flat, the key to the lock turned out to be redundant. The door was ajar. Baffled, we went inside and switched on the light. The apartment had been burgled. There was nothing left inside it, apart from the furniture.

'No, actually, when I say there was nothing left in it, that's not strictly true: laid out carefully on the day bed in the front room, in other words, in the most conspicuous place, was my concert gown, the one I would be performing in the following day; and, next to it, on one side – my shoes, and on the other side – my violin.

'What gallant thieves, so interested in the arts! All that was missing was a little card: "Wishing you good luck."

'It's not difficult to work out how we spent that night. The police, the investigation, etc. There was no question of getting any sleep.

'I messed up in the second round. I let down badly those who were expecting a prize. (I was just given a certificate.) And I didn't even take the edge off their disappointment by telling them what had happened. I didn't defend myself. I didn't say anything to anyone. In this way, I also deprived the journalists of a bombshell moment. How they'd have played that one! It never even entered my mind. I was incredibly impractical.

'Unfortunately, I still don't know how to rid myself of that trait.'[4]

3 Marriage and Recognition

'You take such long strides when you dance!'

Between her second and third trips to Paris, Grażyna found work in the Polish Radio Orchestra, set up and conducted by Grzegorz Fitelberg. She played in the first violin section. This work took up much of her time and energy. Despite the various difficulties or conflicts that often arise when people work as a team, Grażyna honed her orchestration skills during this time. What mattered was that she was earning a modest living. Both sisters, who were now living with their mother, had to be self-reliant. It was hardly surprising, therefore, that an enthusiastic Grażyna, with a multitude of ideas, took the decision to form a string quartet with herself as leader. The second violinist in the quartet was Bohdan Łosakiewicz, who had introduced Grażyna to the man she would marry. Even before the Wieniawski Competition, Bohdan had, quite by chance, brought along his friend Andrzej Biernacki, a 32-year-old medical doctor, to a concert. He was a strapping man with a great sense of humour and extraordinary inner strength. We may imagine that first meeting between Biernacki and Grażyna:

'Andrzej felt a strong handshake, rather too strong for a woman, he thought at the time. She laughed and asked: "Do you really like old Dukas?"

'"Can you imagine *him* dancing with a broom, Grażynko?" Bohdan asked doubtfully.

'"I can, indeed; why not?"

'"He's a serious doctor, who's saving the world."

'"Stop it, my friend; this beautiful woman's going to think that I'm a miserable fellow."

'"So would you know how to fly on a broom?" Grażyna was showing an interest, her blue eyes flashing playfully beneath her dark eyelashes.

'"If you command…"

"'Ooh, you be careful," Bohdan interjected. "This tiny creature has her grip on an entire quartet. Three guys obey her without batting an eyelid."'[6]

The initial flirtation at the time of the memorable competition turned into mutual fascination, and eventually into love.

In one of the letters that Andrzej wrote to Grażyna before their wedding, he recalled their early meetings: 'There was one time I couldn't get to sleep, and I began to recall all the times we met "earlier on". So there I am remembering, remembering, and I suddenly realize that I can remember them much better than anything else that happened at the time. I'm not even thinking of events like the concert at the Conservatoire, or that crazy time at the Adria (I can remember that as if it were today: we were sitting on the shorter side, the one further away from the dance floor, in the loggia, and I was surprised to see that, for a woman, you took such very long strides when you were dancing); or, for instance, when we once met on Mazowiecka Street. We exchanged banalities, but I can remember it as if it were yesterday. I'd meet you at concerts with Bohdan, and I remember that you always had a very masculine kind of handshake; I remember the way you moved, the soft way you pronounced certain words, the power of a single word. Did I realize at the time with whom I was speaking, with whom I was dancing? How strange it is and how delightful!'[2]

In the summer of 1935, they left together for the Mazury region. Andrzej hired a folding canoe and acquired a tent. They stayed in it for the best part of a month, rowing, swimming, and sun-bathing every day. They swam in totally wild Masurian lakes, bought their food from countryside farms, and when it rained, they slept in barns, on hay. The warm, carefree summer, with its dreams of a future together, passed quickly by. In the late autumn, the couple had to part. Andrzej had been awarded a scholarship from the Jakub Potocki Foundation and he left for a year's study abroad. First he travelled to Vienna, then to Rome, to the Carlo Forlanini Institute; from there he went on to Davos, Paris, Szczecin, and finally Berlin. He neither could nor wanted to turn down the scholarship. He was ambitious but, above all, he wanted to become a better doctor. His departure gave the two of them many sleepless nights.

For Andrzej, this was a very important step in his medical career. Ten years earlier, in 1925, while a student, he had studied at the Pasteur Institute in Paris. He had finished his medical studies at the University of Warsaw in 1928. The following year he had gone out to Brazil, to the Orzeł Biały (White Eagle) Polish colony in the state of Espirito Santo, where he had helped the local population and collected material on the health conditions in the area. Travel was in his blood.

'What a terrible thing distance is!'

On 21 November 1935, Grażyna accompanied Andrzej to the railway station, and for a long time stood watching as the Vienna-bound train, wreathed in puffs of grey smoke, left Warsaw and disappeared into the distance. She held herself together bravely and never cried in public. Only on her return home did she begin to feel uneasy. Once she had sat down in front of a sheet of writing paper, she understood that there were 365 lonely days before her. How many minutes was that? – 525,600; in other words, 31,536,000 seconds. She worked it out in her head as she wrote her first letter to Andrzej – one of many that they exchanged at that time. The letters have survived, thanks to Wanda's foresight, as she packed them in a suitcase, along with Grażyna's compositions. This suitcase was in their apartment, and fortunately was taken along at the last moment when the family left Warsaw during the Second World War. In fact, they left twice: once in 1939 and again in 1944.

Within months, both Grażyna and Andrzej were missing each other a great deal. In March 1936, Andrzej wrote a letter from Rome: 'I don't for a single moment, think in bourgeois terms – dosh, career, that kind of thing – nothing of the kind! I just think about our, or rather your happiness. Here abroad, I'm turning myself into a better medical machine (let's say, somewhat pathetically, a social one!). I've been studying a lot, carrying out research. Would I have been able to do that back home? Nearly all of it, but at a considerably slower pace, *au ralenti*. Would I have been able to do it later? Certainly not. This is my last chance to have an extended period of travel. They don't give scholarships to old fellows! Do you not think that there might have come a time when you'd have regarded me somewhat differently: you, who are constantly developing so much, if I had just stayed at the level of a mediocrity?'[2]

During their enforced separation, Grażyna succumbed to doubt on a few occasions. Their joint future from the perspective of a faraway Warsaw seemed hazy to her. She gave way to her emotions and conveyed her fears in the letters she wrote. No sooner had she taken one of Andrzej's anxiety-filled letters about their joint future out of the mailbox, than she would quickly seize hold of her pen and hurriedly explain: 'You see: I'm a person who's prone to extremes. Just as I love you without measure, in the same way I easily fall into despair without measure on your account. Everything in general in my life is greatly exaggerated. I do hope that you'll cure me of this one day, when we're living together – obviously excepting my love for you... All these things come from my boundless longing for you. I know that you long for me too, but it seems that you're able to do your longing in a calm way. The way I do my longing is killing me. You could in fact accuse me of selfishness. It seems like a whim of mine that I'm demanding a swifter return from you – that I don't care about your matters – but I promise you that this is not through selfishness, when you know that I regard my own matters as absolutely nothing compared to, for instance, meeting up with you. I would very willingly give up five years of my composing, which is apparently important to me, to be with you at least a month sooner. So that's why I was so desperately sad when I saw from your letters how you feel quite differently, that you can rise above these things and carry on with everyday matters. People have, in fact, really made a mess-up of life. What's really meaningful in life is seen as being of lesser importance, and the other way around; our silly activities which, after all, are only important on the surface, we regard as the very essence of life.'[2]

Meanwhile, writing from Rome, an ever-calm and level-headed Andrzej appealed to Grażyna: 'My dearest! What a terrible thing distance is! I now think that this is the main reason for all my (and maybe yours too) anxieties and worries… I'm writing you one letter at the same time as you're writing me another. I'm receiving and replying to a letter at the same time as you're receiving and replying to something entirely different; it's enough to drive one mad!'[2]

Success or 'paradox'?

Grażyna kept her despondency at bay by undertaking lots of activities and duties. She would hurry to her quartet practices, which took place in Andrzej's apartment on Kopernika Street; then she would rush off to rehearsals and concerts with the Polish Radio Orchestra. She composed mainly by night, which led to her feeling overworked.

The prizes and nominations that she received at the time helped her to set aside her longing. Her *Trio* for oboe, violin, and cello was awarded second prize in the Association of Polish Music Publishers composition competition. It was performed in March 1936 at the Conservatoire at a promotional concert in which Prokofiev took part. Wanda found a review of the concert in the latest edition of the newspaper, *Nowiny Codzienne* (*The Daily News*).[11]

'Do you know what Michał Kondracki has written about the concert?' she asked Grażyna with a smile.

'I have no idea, Wandziu,' replied her sister, hurriedly drinking her morning coffee.

'That "the best piece in this concert (it sounds like a paradox!) was the *Trio* for oboe, violin, and cello by the young Grażyna Bacewicz, as performed by Śnieckowski, Kmitowa, and Halber. One cannot assume, however, that this exceptionally talented, most promising of composers will necessarily match people like, for example, Hindemith or Prokofiev in terms of the extent of her inspiration or creative value. She does, however, have very many interesting ideas, a freshness of invention (especially in the first and original *cantilena*), and a kind of endearing sincerity in the way she expresses herself. One has the impression that, for her, creativity is an inner need, almost a compulsion and a force of nature. Let's hope she really flourishes, matures, thinks a good deal and critically so, works and analyses; in other words, does not dash the hopes that we have for her after having heard the beautiful *Adagio, Allegro,* and *Vivace* of her *Trio*."[11]

It annoyed Grażyna that she should have to prove her worth in relation to men. After all, she was every bit as good as her fellow male composers; they should not be treating her with condescension.

'Don't you think that women are in no way inferior to men when it comes to composition?' she said belligerently, placing her cup back on its saucer.

'Well of course!' Wanda exclaimed, giving the newspaper a vigorous shake.

'You know, it's becoming increasingly clear to me that if a woman who deals with men all the time wants to be respected, she has to put on airs and graces. It's a pity that's not in my nature. Maybe I can manage to develop some fake self-importance. That's the best medicine for men,' said Grażyna, planting a kiss on her sister's cheek by way of good-bye.

That day was as full of activities as the previous one, and all the days that followed, until Andrzej returned.

On 15 March 1936, in the same competition, Grażyna Bacewicz also received a commendation for another composition. She immediately shared the good news with her fiancé: 'I had a wonderful day yesterday. The *Sinfonietta* turned out to be excellent. You do know how self-critical I am, but in this case, I really don't have anything to berate myself for. Whereas after composing the *Trio*, I thought it was very good, but on hearing it played, I only rated the third movement. Well, with the *Sinfonietta*, after I'd composed it, it seemed to me to have shortcomings, but on hearing it, I thought it was excellent. You know, I really listened to this thing as if it weren't mine, but as if it had been written by some other very clever composer. In fact, I can't believe that it was I who wrote it. It's awfully lively, cheerful, witty, with not one second of bagginess. In fact, I don't really understand how this pessimism-on-legs that I am at present, can write such cheery music. Ficio* really likes it: nothing but superlatives; the same from those listening. My colleagues made a real effort.'[2]

'As regards the wedding…'

In the spring, Grażyna began looking for an apartment for herself and Andrzej to live in after their wedding. In her letters she gave her fiancé an account of her search. After various twists and turns, she took a rented apartment at 35 Koszykowa Street, which would be their home for the next 26 years. This was where their daughter Alina was born during World War II.

On 8 July 1936, Grażyna wrote: 'As regards the wedding, friends are out of the question. It's a mere formality, after all. Your parents, Miecio [Andrzej's

---

* Translator's note: 'Ficio' is Grażyna Bacewicz's pet name for the conductor, Grzegorz Fitelberg.

brother], my mother, Wanda, Kiejstut, Bohdan, and that's it! Right? We can send out some little printed bits of paper to our friends later on, to let them know that we've got married, reading more or less as follows: "Grażyna Bacewicz and Andrzej Biernacki are pleased to inform you that their marriage took place on such and such a day." I think that by convention, your name should come first, but it seems that's not appropriate here. Anyway, you edit it – that would be best. Safe journey to Berlin… Have you remembered about the strings and the rosin? What about the ties? Write lots! It's only 26 days to go. But I have in fact forgotten to write about what lies closest to my heart. Miecio writes that you've lost weight. Why? What reason? Shape up! All my love.'[2]

Meanwhile in Europe, there was a growing fear of war. On his way back to Warsaw, Andrzej found himself in Berlin on the opening day of the Olympics: 1 August 1936. In a letter to his fiancée, he described in detail what went on that day on the streets of the city. 'Terrible crowds, but just Germans… At first, a whole procession of top hats from assorted committees arrived. Then Hess, then Göring, then Hitler, standing in a car and smiling like a deity on holiday. A guy ran past with that "flame" in his hand; just in case, they also had another two ready-lit "flames" being driven along in a car; and he raced to the stadium to light the Olympic flame. As soon as that had taken place, "the Handsome Adolf" let rip with a speech that even I could have managed after two vodkas (I've forgotten I don't drink!) but that gave rise to mass uproar. Shortly afterwards, they went hell for leather with an anthem (obviously an Olympic one again), composed, incidentally, by R. Strauss. A good job, as you'd expect with Strauss, but not exactly *Don Juan*. There's something hollow about it. I didn't like it! Then more noise and it was over.'[2]

A few days later, on 6 August 1936, Grażyna and Andrzej got married in St Alexander's Church in Warsaw. It was a modest family celebration. Straight after the reception, which Grażyna's sister and mother had organized at the apartment in Koszykowa Street, the young couple took the evening train for their honeymoon in Zalishchyky.*

'The first violin concerto to have been composed by a woman'

When she returned from her honeymoon, Grażyna went back to composing and playing in the orchestra. On 21 October 1936, at the Polish Society for Contemporary Music, the singer Stanisława Korwin-Szymanowska stood up

---

*   Translator's note: The city of Zalishchyky has been under different rule at different times in its history. In 1936, the city was within the Polish Republic and was known as 'Zaleszczyki'. It was a very popular spa town with a direct rail connection to Warsaw and was nicknamed the 'Polish Riviera'. The city is now in western Ukraine.

on stage and, in her beautiful voice, sang Grażyna's song, *Mów do mnie o miły* (*Speak to me, my love!*) to words by Rabindranath Tagore, as translated by Jan Kasprowicz. She was accompanied on the piano by Kiejstut Bacewicz. This was an unusual event, given that in the composer's oeuvre, there are barely a dozen or so songs.

In 1937 Grażyna composed her first violin concerto, and a year later she took part in its premiere, on 28 March 1938. She played the solo violin part herself, accompanied by the Polish Radio Orchestra, conducted by its director, Grzegorz Fitelberg. The concerto had a classical structure, with three movements, although it did not have any solo cadenzas. The orchestra carried on a dialogue with the solo instrument, emphasizing the delicacy of the narrative, but there were also loud moments from the brass.

'The first violin concerto to have been composed by a woman!' thundered the newspaper headlines, embellished with a photo of Grażyna.

The political background to these artistic events continued to be one of unrest. From its very beginning, the year 1938 had not been an easy one. On 12 March, on Hitler's orders, the *Wehrmacht* entered Austria, implementing Plan Otto; tens of thousands of *Wehrmacht* soldiers, police personnel, members of the *SS*, as well as air units took part in the action.* Adolf Hitler himself arrived in Austria. On 13 March 1938, the Austrian Nazis announced new legislation, which brought Austria into the German Reich and named it Ostmark. To legitimize the annexation of Austria, a referendum was held on 10 April 1938. The official announcement left no doubt: 99 per cent of those who participated in the referendum in Germany had voted 'yes' to Austria being incorporated in the German Reich; the figure in Austria was 99.7 per cent. Shortly after, both the United Kingdom and France acknowledged the Greater German Reich.

Rue Lamandé third time around

Around this time, encouraged by her husband, Grażyna resigned her position with the Polish Radio Orchestra and set off for the refreshing air of Paris. On the Rue Lamandé, she met up with other Polish musicians. Amongst them were Antoni Szałowski, the pianist Wanda Łosakiewicz, Michał Spisak, Witold Rudziński, Czesław Lewicki, Andrzej Panufnik, Roman Palester, Jerzy Fitelberg and, eventually, Stefan Kisielewski. They were all friends. During the daytime they would work intensively, and in the evenings, they would go out on the town. On occasion, Grażyna, with a group of her friends, would go dancing

---

* Translator's note: The *Wehrmacht* were the unified armed forces of Nazi Germany, the Nazis being members of the far-right Nationalist Socialist German Workers' Party. The *SS* (Schutzstaffel ['Protective Echelon' in German]) were the black-uniformed elite political corps of the Nazi Party.

in a club on Rue Vaugirard. The École Normale de Musique still had the strict and meticulous Mademoiselle Nadia Boulanger teaching there.

Grażyna exchanged quite a few letters with the family in Warsaw. On Christmas Day 1938, she wrote to her husband: 'I spent Christmas Eve on my own, but that's how I wanted it. I went to the cinema. Everything was open here. Obviously, I told my friends that I'd been invited elsewhere for Christmas Eve. I didn't feel at all sad. I'll be going out to dinner in a minute with Wanda [Łosakiewicz], and then later to her aunt's. In the evening I'll be going to see an American play, which only has women performing in it.'[2]

At the start of the year 1939, Grażyna began organizing a concert of her own works, and this took up a great deal of her time and energy. She was busy composing new pieces and was viewing Poland from afar. What she was reading in the newspapers about the tense international situation was causing her increasing worry.

'Dear Andrzej! Will you write and tell me exactly why there have been demonstrations in Poland against the Germans? About Gdańsk – what have they done now? I read here that there have been horrid notices in restaurants in Gdańsk, that Poles and pigs have been forbidden entry. Did that happen? Yesterday I managed to wangle my way into a radio concert. (There were no tickets, it was invitation only.) There was Roussel's *Symphony No. 4*, which we've played, and which I like very much; after that, Bartók (who's prowling around Paris at the moment) was meant to be playing his *Concerto No. II* with orchestra, but as the sheet music didn't arrive in time, he played some of his old piano pieces – dull, however. Bartók's most interesting stuff is his most recent, after all. I'm glad that I still have another ten years to develop. Once you get to forty, you have to have created something decidedly good. Later we heard Stravinsky's *Four Studies* for orchestra – very interesting (I wasn't familiar with them) and Hindemith's *Noblissima* for orchestra; but it wasn't terribly so.'[2]

On 18 March, two days after the Protectorate of Bohemia and Moravia, a puppet state controlled by the Nazis, was set up, Grażyna wrote to her husband: 'My concert matters have fallen into a rut due to illness, and I just don't know what to do. The Czech business has really upset me. I do feel sorry for them. The saddest thing about all of this is the fact that not one state has so much as said a word. Which means that Hitler can do whatever he wants. The outlook's not great for us either. Gdańsk is one thing, but it could get worse. I can imagine how upset my father is about Klaipėda. I've seen the Germans entering Czechoslovakia at the cinema, and the atmosphere on the second day in the towns and the villages – everybody crying. I can't quite understand how there's no-one to be found who would bump Hitler off.'[2]

'I played just brilliantly'

Her 'composer's concert', for which Grażyna had received funding from the Polish Embassy in Paris, took place on 26 April 1939 in the concert hall of the École Normale de Musique. As well as the premiere of her newly-composed *String Quartet No. 1* and her *Piano Sonata No. 2* (which she later withdrew from her catalogue), the programme included her *Trio* for oboe, violin, and cello, *Theme and Variations*, *Lithuanian Song*, *Partita for Violin and Piano*, *Children's Suite*, *Scherzo for Piano*, and finally, her *Sonata for Oboe and Piano*. Among the performers were Le Quatuor Figueroa and the oboist Louis Bleuzet.

In a letter to her sister and mother which she wrote as soon as she got back to Rue Lamandé, Grażyna described exactly how the event had gone: 'I arrived at the concert with Wanda Ł.[osakiewicz]. I was actually in a rather apathetic state of mind, and my hands were cold, as it was a very chilly day. My dress looked very good. I didn't wear a bra, as my bust's still up to the job. All the soloists behaved very respectfully towards me. The cellist from the quartet exceptionally so! Very handsome and lovely. It started fifteen minutes late, in other words, at a quarter past nine. I didn't hear the *Trio* or the *Piano Sonata* because I had to warm up, but even so I still went on with cold hands, though suddenly, once I was up on stage, my stage fright disappeared. I played incredibly calmly, just brilliantly. There was a surprising number of people there for that kind of concert: around three hundred. I'd only expected to see fifty people. It's a small concert hall, so it looked great. Lechoń* arrived after the first half, with lots of people. Lechoń told me that Florent Schmitt's there, and that he's saying he must come to my room to see me, to see whether I'm nice looking… My *Sonata* for oboe and piano came out well. The best, of course, was the *Quartet*.

'After the concert Schmitt did come to see me, and as I was wearing furs, he told me to remove them, which I did, of course. He asked me where I'd had my dress made, so I told him it was a Parisian gown, and then he seemed upset that it wasn't from Warsaw. Later he said that he liked the second and third movements of the *Quartet* very much. It does indeed sound very good. Loads of people kept coming to see me. Everyone was delighted that it had gone so well. Composer's concerts are generally not particularly successful. Lechoń was also very pleased, and I don't think he regrets the Embassy having stumped up the cash. After the *Quartet*, I had to go out and take another bow. In a word – a real triumph! It was incredible! The pianist took the *Children's Suite* away with him, because he wants to play it on the radio, and the *Scherzo*.

---

* Translator's note: Jan Lechoń (1899–1956) was a Polish poet, literary and theatre critic and co-founder of the literary group Skamander and the Polish Institute of Arts and Sciences of America. From 1930 to 1939 he was Cultural Attaché at the Polish Embassy in Paris.

We'll have to see what F. Schmitt writes, but I don't think it's going to be bad.'[2]

An approaching threat

Not long after her composer's concert, Grażyna returned to Warsaw. Had she received a scholarship for further study, she would probably have extended her stay in Paris until November 1939. When she received news that she had been turned down, what else could she do but pack her suitcases and say goodbye to the residents of the house in Rue Lamandé? By May 1939 she was back in Warsaw. Husband and wife spent a hot July in the village of Marynin, just outside Lublin, in Andrzej's aunt's house. Away from the capital, people did not feel the growing international tension. The sunny summer was filling them with optimism. Everyone was hoping that war wouldn't happen. However, when on 24 August, now back in Warsaw, Grażyna heard the piercing wail of the air-raid siren, she was overcome by fear and an inner trembling that was difficult to control. Shortly afterwards, that same day, the radio broadcast an appeal by the city's mayor, Stefan Starzyński, in which he urged the citizens of Warsaw to dig ditches for anti-aircraft artillery.

The signs of an approaching threat did not, however, interfere with the daily entertainment of the Varsovians. Despite the tension, life carried on at its usual pace. The following day, anyone who fancied it, could pop into the Europa Cinema on Nowy Świat Street to see the film première of *The Story of Vernon and Irene Castle** with Fred Astaire and Ginger Rogers. The Bałtyk Cinema on Chmielna Street was showing Walter Lang and William A. Seiter's *The Little Princess* with Shirley Temple in the lead role. On their way home after a show, people could not fail to notice the posters that had gone up on walls around the city, with photos of the Commander-in-Chief Edward Śmigły-Rydz, and the battle cry: 'Violence inflicted by force must be fought off with force. We will not give in; we will overcome our assailant.' Passers-by would stop and stand in front of the posters, looking at the drawings of columns of soldiers, tanks, and bomber planes. People were queuing in front of shops for sugar, flour, and preserves. Soap stores and drug stores were running out of kerosene, candles, and soap. People were desperate to buy paper strips to secure their windows.

On 30 August 1939, an announcement was made about general mobilization. Streets, railway stations, and cafes began teeming with excited crowds. The movement of long-distance trains was restricted, so travellers became stuck at railway stations. On the night of 31 August 1939, all the trams and buses in the city ceased to run.

---

*   Translator's note: The title of the movie in Polish translates as *On Wings*.

4 War and Resistance

'Before our very eyes'

The first bombs fell in the suburbs of Warsaw at dawn on 1 September 1939. That morning, the news bulletin on the radio announced that at 4.45 a.m. the German army had invaded Poland. The city was gripped with excitement; men in uniform headed for the railway stations. Most shops were open, and there was no sense of panic. On Saturday, 2 September 1939, the Germans launched a particularly heavy attack on Warsaw. There were repeated air attacks throughout the day. The radio was constantly broadcasting warnings: 'This is an air raid alarm for the city of Warsaw.' News spread by word of mouth about the defence of Westerplatte.

On 3 September 1939, the *Warsaw Courier* ran an article about 'The deal between two totalitarian regimes' in which it described the new alliance forged between the Germans and the Soviets. This fact was tempered that same afternoon by the news that the United Kingdom and France had declared war on Germany. There was a collective sigh of relief from all those huddled around radio sets. Crowds began to gather outside the British Embassy on Nowy Świat Street and the French Embassy on Frascati Street.

On 4 September 1939 air attacks set off fires in the centres of the Praga and Grochów districts of Warsaw. Factory buildings in the Wola area went up in flames. On 5 September 1939, while German bombs fell on the Eastern Railway Station, large numbers of people evacuated from the western territories had begun arriving in Warsaw. Hungry, exhausted, and frightened, these travellers had miraculously escaped the German air attacks. It was said that the Stuka dive-bombers were even firing at columns of refugees, who were walking along the roads leading into Warsaw. The queues in front of the shops were starting to get longer, but there were no food shortages as yet. On 6 September 1939, the Mayor of Warsaw, Stefan Starzyński, gave the directive for a Civic Guard to be set up as a social structure for maintaining order. That afternoon there was heavy bombing of bridges: notably the Średnicowy and Poniatowski Bridges. Bombs destroyed the ammunition depots in Palmiry (to the north of Warsaw). The nearby forest caught fire. A thick curtain of black smoke hung over the city. That evening, on the radio, Varsovians heard a statement from the then Polish prime minister, Sławoj Składkowski. An assertive voice announced: 'On account of the danger that threatens the city, the Government has been forced to leave Warsaw, with the steadfast intention of returning once war has been won.'

Men were called up and instructed to march eastwards. Before dawn, thousands of reservists and entire families were leaving the city. Walking among the crowds of refugees were members of the Bacewicz family. At the very last moment, Grażyna had grabbed the suitcase filled with her compositions, letters, and important paperwork, and then run out of the Koszykowa Street apartment. Her husband and brother had decided to accompany the women to Marynin, and then join the war against the Germans.

What happened next is described by Grażyna in her short story, '*Na naszych oczach*' ('Before Our Very Eyes'): 'As the men were, in any case, obliged to head out east, we all set off. After a dozen or so hours on the road to Lublin, an ordeal that those who experienced (and there were huge, massed crowds of people) will certainly remember for the rest of their lives, we eventually found ourselves in Garwolin.

'Along with other refugees, we headed for the barracks, where they were selling grain coffee and bread rolls.

'Members of my family tucked into the food. They were treating the infirmary as a refuge. They were clearly intending to rest there. I managed to down a few mouthfuls, but then I suddenly started shaking again, as I had done during the bombing. I began to snatch my family's unfinished cups of coffee out of their hands and, in a rather (I admit) strange-sounding voice, I kept repeating: "Let's get out of here! Now – let's get out!"

'My husband, a doctor, a calm person, was pretending that he couldn't see what I was up to. My brother, Kiejstut – always extremely accommodating of other people's weaknesses – patiently advised me to try to calm down. My sister, Wanda was smiling warmly, trying to give me some extra courage. My sister-in-law – pale and exhausted – was rubbing her aching legs. My mother, after our recent ordeals, had no intention of making any comments regarding my "moods".

'The strategy of these five people failed. In my "cowardice", I turned out to be stronger than all of them.

'"Can't you understand? We have to get out of here right now!" I was shaking more and more, even starting to tear the hair out of my head. I think it was this last thing that was the deciding factor. My husband whispered to my brother and they gave way (they didn't have a straitjacket with them, after all).

'I thought all five of them were walking too slowly.

'"Faster, faster, move it!" I kept hurrying them on.

"'Will you just calm down!"
'These domineering words of my husband's might, on another occasion, have made some impression on me; this time, however, they fell on deaf ears. "Run!" I kept yelling. "Oh, there's the bridge. We have to get across to the other side!"

'Barely had I achieved my aim – in other words, corralled my little brood over to the other side of the bridge – than we heard the characteristic whirr of the bombers. Of a whole squadron of them.

'A few minutes later, Garwolin ceased to exist. That happened before our very eyes.'[4]

On reaching Marynin and making sure that the women were safe there, Kiejstut and Andrzej volunteered for the army. As a doctor, Andrzej would be working in army hospitals in Zamość, Złoczów, and Lwów [now Lviv].

Capitulation and occupation of Warsaw

On 1 October 1939, a Sunday, the Germans occupied the whole of Warsaw. They took over the state buildings on Szucha Avenue; at number 23 they set up the headquarters of Hitler's police, and a few days later, the Chancellor of the Reich, Adolf Hitler himself, received the victory parade of the German troops, standing on a rostrum on the even-numbered side of Ujazdowskie Avenue, between Na Rozdrożu Square and Piękna Street.

The Bacewicz family returned to the city. Grażyna and Andrzej's home in Koszykowa Street had survived the bombing, as had the building in Mokotowska Street, where Grażyna's mother and sister were living. Most of the city was reduced to rubble.

Throughout October 1939, the streets of Warsaw were frantically being cleared of rubble. The first ones to be cleared were the city's main arteries: Marszałkowska Street and Nowy Świat Street. Before public transport got going again, only horse carts and carriages rode through the streets. From 10 October 1939, water from the city's water hydrants could be accessed free of charge. Rationing of staple foods was introduced.

The eleventh of October 1939 saw the first edition of the *Nowy Kurier Warszawski* (*New Polish Courier*), a Nazi newspaper printed in Polish, which the Poles referred to as 'the rag'. A few days later, some post offices were opened, and the Warsaw Gasworks lit up certain streets. Eventually, the city's power station reconnected electrical supplies, and the apartment in Koszykowa Street was lit by a weak light bulb.

A good friend of the Bacewiczes, the music director of Polish Radio, Edmund Rudnicki, displayed both courage and cunning when he hid all the station's technical equipment after capitulation, having received the order to close down the radio station. He also managed to hide recordings of speeches by Warsaw's Mayor, Stefan Starzyński, that the Germans were trying to get their hands on, as well as manuscripts by Chopin and Szymanowski. He stored the radio equipment in the attic of a building at number 5 Mazowiecka Street. An artists' café, the Arria, which was located on the ground floor at the same address, provided excellent cover with the constant activity in and around the building.

Varsovians hit on the excellent idea of opening 'artistic cafes'; this enabled them to get round any German orders that had been specifically designed to dismantle the musical life of the city. Concert halls ceased to exist. The Philharmonic concert hall and opera house had been bombed, and the music conservatoire had been shut down. Cafes now made performing possible, but musicians had to apply to the German authorities for an *Erlaubnisskarte*, a document that gave them official permission to practise their profession. By 16 November 1939, the Dom Sztuki (Art House) café at 27 Nowy Świat Street (later known as 'Professor Woytowicz's Café') had started putting on concerts. Tickets were not required, but people had to pay for coffee or cake.

Small theatres were also operating. Grażyna's brother, Kiejstut, found his first job in one of these, the Scala, where he accompanied actors and played the music for the shows. After this place was shut down, he moved to the Nowości Theatre and later took a job at the Maska. Like other musicians, he would sign a month's contract, which was the usual requirement.

A representative of the clandestine Musicians' Union, Edmund Rudnicki encouraged musicians to perform at Bolesław Woytowicz's, since it offered the opportunity of 'good' papers. Similarly, permission was sometimes granted to perform in Adam Dołżycki's orchestra, which played at Lardelli's café, although this particular conductor did not have a good reputation. As time went by, he increasingly cooperated with the German authorities, and some claimed that he had declared himself to be a Ukrainian.

Since the beginning of the occupation, artists had been organizing themselves into musical groups. In December 1939, Kazimierz Wiłkomirski and his sister Maria, along with Eugenia Umińska, set up the Wiłkomirski-Umińska Trio. Their first performances took place at the SiM (Sztuka i Moda – Art and Fashion) café on Królewska Street. This was not a large place, but it was an exclusive one. They also played in the Zachęta café until the German propaganda department closed it down. In August 1940, the trio began performing regularly at Woytowicz's café. The trio proved to be a success and decided to branch out. In February 1941, Umińska and Wiłkomirski, along with Roman Padlewski and Henryk Trzonek, set up the Umińska Quartet. Every Sunday at Woytowicz's saw the trio performing, and every Thursday the quartet.

So as not to get caught out by German propaganda, artists made difficult choices. The occupying German authorities kept issuing new directives, restrictions, and repressive measures that were burdensome to the Polish artists. On occasion the Germans would put artists' names on posters without their permission.

Eugenia Umińska was given one such 'order' in the autumn of 1942. She saw her name on a poster for a symphony concert conducted by Albert Hösl. Not long before that, the Wiłkomirski-Umińska Trio had refused to perform at a private concert for the Governor of the District of Radom. That was when someone had informed on Eugenia Umińska, revealing that she belonged to the resistance movement. Edmund Rudnicki immediately went into action. He contacted the composer and alpinist Wawrzyniec Żuławski, who in turn contacted a certain Austrian (now a Gestapo employee), a man he had met on a mountaineering expedition before the war. On receiving the request from Żuławski, the said Gestapo mountaineer destroyed the information from the informer, but it became clear that if on this occasion Eugenia Umińska were not to perform for the Germans, she would have to disappear from Warsaw for some time. Which is, in fact, what happened.

A little daughter

By 1941 Grażyna had become so used to the reality of war that she had gone back to composing. She wrote her *Sonata* for solo violin (unnumbered) and *Three Preludes for Piano*. She performed the premieres of both pieces in 1941 at underground concerts. In 1942 she organized musical evenings at home in her apartment. In July of that year, she gave birth to a little daughter, Alina. It was so much easier for the young mother to invite guests to her home than to leave her child behind and rush out to a concert, especially as going out would put her at risk of being caught up in a round-up or control check by the Germans.

The child was born in the apartment on Koszykowa Street. She was named 'Alina', after a character in Słowacki's *Balladyna*.*

'In the early hours of twenty-first August 1942, when Grażyna's daughter was just a month old, Soviet aeroplanes dropped illumination flares on parachutes onto the city. Huge lanterns fell soundlessly, melting the empty streets and squares with an unearthly flash. Grażyna was woken by the wailing of the air-raid sirens. She pulled back the blanket that had been blacking out the windows and looked out at the brightly lit sky. The baby was lying on the bed. She had just stopped crying and had fallen asleep. The little one was suffering from hunger, as Grażyna did not have much breast milk. Her tiny fists kept opening and closing, and as she slept, her lips suckled on the non-existent milk.'[12]

They had to seek refuge in the basement. All hunched up there, the women listened to the noise of falling bombs and the firing of German anti-aircraft artillery.

---

* Translator's note: *Balladyna* is a play by the nineteenth-century playwright, Juliusz Słowacki (1809–1849). Alina is Balladyna's kind-hearted younger sister.

The following day, Grażyna decided to leave for Marynin. From there she wrote to her husband: 'We're all fine. The little one's healthy. She's eating a huge amount. We had one tragic day when I had too little milk, and the little one screamed all day long at the top of her voice. I felt so terribly sorry for her. I asked for more fluids, and I bought some bread, which made Auntie cross with me for one day, but everything's fine now with Auntie, and I have a bit of bread in my room, and I've been stuffing myself with it, with disgust, for the sake of our little daughter. Although it's cold, the Little One gets out into the fresh air every day.'

Then, on 21 September, Grażyna wrote saying: 'Our little daughter…was two months old yesterday, so I sat her on the settee (Wanda will tell you how funny she is when she's sitting there) and we all congratulated her. Then we had the ceremonial weighing. It's hardly surprising that the little one's been pumping away at her mother for all she's worth, as she's gaining weight beautifully. Last time she weighed 4.28 [kilos], and now she's at 4.67, so she's put on 39 decagrams within eleven days – not bad at all, right?'[2]

Uprising in the ghetto

On 2 October 1940, when Governor Ludwig Fischer had signed the order to create a ghetto for the Jewish population of Warsaw, tens of thousands of people had been forced to relocate. Poles were ordered to leave the designated territory, while the Jews had to move out of the Aryan side. They were only allowed to take a 'refugee bundle' – bedding and personal items – as hand luggage. On the streets that marked the ghetto boundary, tall red-brick walls were hurriedly erected. On 16 November 1940, the ghetto gates were closed. The ghetto district was surrounded by a police cordon; no-one was allowed to leave without a pass. Trams that were run under the German-controlled 'Blue Police' surveillance cut through the ghetto without stopping.

Hunger and illness plagued the people who were locked up in what was the largest ghetto to have been created by the Germans in the whole of occupied Europe. On 13 February 1943 musician friends of Grażyna's heard that Władysław Szpilman had managed to get out of the ghetto thanks to Janina and Andrzej Boguccy. By the end of the war, nearly thirty people in Warsaw had helped him survive in hiding, among whom were Edmund Rudnicki, Piotr Perkowski, Eugenia Umińska, and Witold Lutosławski.

When at dawn on 19 April 1943, a heavy SS unit approaching from the direction of Nalewki Street entered through the ghetto gate, followed by a tank and two armoured vehicles, the Jews launched an unexpected attack from the corners of Nalewki, Gęsia, Miła, and Zamenhofa streets. With the help of grenades and Molotov cocktails, members of the Jewish Combat Association torched the tank and killed twelve Germans, forcing them to turn back. The ghetto uprising had begun.

On 21 April 1943, the sky above the whole ghetto was aglow with fire. Thick clouds of black smoke hovered above the city. The Germans systematically torched building after building, throwing smoke bombs into cellars and sewers, forcing the combatants to flee the burning buildings.

'People are being burned to death, jumping out of windows onto duvets and pillows that they've thrown out, so as not to surrender to the Germans,' went the admiring whispers.

With concern and trepidation, Grażyna and her mother and sister followed the accounts they heard of ongoing battles. The situation in the city was desperate. Jews were being captured on the streets, including on the Aryan side, and executed on the spot.

On the night of 12 May 1943, a Soviet long-range bomber began dropping illumination flares, and then launched a full-blown bombing attack. Grażyna, her baby in her arms, her sister, Wanda, and their mother, all ran down to the cellar. The shelter began filling up with people.

Exploding incendiary bombs were falling on the city in thick bursts. The booms were coming nearer and nearer. The building was shaking with every explosion, and rattling in an alarming fashion. Rubble was falling from the ceiling. Grażyna closed her eyes and covered her baby's face with her hand.

'They've hit the annexe!' someone shouted.

'Let's get out!'

As they scrambled out of the shelter, they saw piles of rubble. The flickering glare of a fire lit up the courtyard, which looked like the hell of a Hieronymus Bosch painting. It took a long time for the women to calm down.

That night, bombs had fallen on Marszałkowska Street, by Zbawiciela Square, in Jerozolimskie Avenue, on Grójecka Street, in the Okęcie area, and onto the railway lines. Buildings had been burned down in Emilia Plater Street, as had the market hall on Koszykowa Street and two buildings on the corner of Koszykowa Street and Marszałkowska Street. Overturned trams and smouldering ruins were piled high in the streets. The following morning, everything was covered by a thick layer of dust; small carts with passengers were rattling through the streets. People were pulling handcarts with their rescued belongings.

Grażyna's family had been extraordinarily lucky. Their home on Koszykowa Street had survived the Soviet bombings intact.

Clandestine concerts

The twenty-first of May 1943 saw the premiere of Grażyna Bacewicz's *String Quartet No. 2* take place in Woytowicz's café.

The performers went up on stage. Eugenia Umińska, as usual, was looking extremely elegant; the viola player, Henryk Trzonek, was glancing carefully around the room; Tadeusz Ochlewski (second violin) was bowing with concentration, while Kazimierz Wiłkomirski, holding his cello, was winking knowingly at Grażyna.

The composer had not yet heard her own composition, other than in her imagination. She became completely immersed in the music. She had based her piece on the principle of contrast between movements. She had found writing the middle movement, the *Andante*, most rewarding. There, she had let her creativity flow freely, and the ideas had come of their own accord, naturally. The two outer movements – the *Allegro ma non troppo* and the *Allegro* – had a lively and busy sound. At one point she picked up a re-worked echo of a folk song that she had heard somewhere in the countryside. The theme altered in a subtle way, and the emotions surged. She had juxtaposed two strong chords at the beginning to good effect: a combination of E major with A major and B major with F sharp major.

When applause followed the final *Allegro*, Eugenia, with an animated gesture, invited Grażyna up onto the stage. Grażyna mounted the steps in a hurry and gave a quick, manly, bow.

The day after the concert, the Gestapo arrived at the café and arrested the owner, Bolesław Woytowicz. By some miracle he was eventually released, but only after spending a whole month in Pawiak Prison. The café was closed for a few weeks.

That same year, Eugenia Umińska and Irena Dubiska performed the premiere of Grażyna Bacewicz's *Suite for Two Violins*. Clandestine concerts were obviously surrounded by secrecy. People would arrive at these events in pairs and slip unnoticed through the gate of the building, so as not to draw the Germans' attention. Chairs were placed along the walls of the room and in the entrance hall. In a private space like this, the music sounded louder than normal, as if it were trying to drown out the sound of the distant grenade explosions in the ghetto area. The audience listened intently to the two violinists, Umińska and Dubiska, but no-one dared clap at the end. People made their congratulations in silence, through smiles and a squeeze of the hand, and then they went back out into the street two by two. So passed another concert organized by the Central Welfare Council.*

At a distance once again

As fate would have it, in the summer of 1943, Andrzej fell ill with tuberculosis. He was initially treated at the sanatorium in Otwock, then later in Marynin. At that same time, he was also writing up his postdoctoral thesis. It is likely that

---

* Translator's note: The Central Welfare Council, known as the Rada Główna Opiekuńcza (RGO) was one of the few charities that was allowed to operate during the German occupation of Poland. Its main purpose was to provide relief to homeless, orphaned, and displaced people.

he only returned to his medical duties at the No. 2 Clinic for Internal Diseases at the start of 1944. He presented a lecture on his postdoctoral research before the Board of the Underground Faculty of Medicine at the University of Warsaw and was consequently awarded the title of Associate Professor for Pathology and In-Depth Treatment of Internal Diseases.

Grażyna, who could not rely on any financial contribution from her husband while he was ill, ran the household with Wanda's help. She wanted to make provision to support her family through the coming wartime winter, so, towards the end of August, she asked Professor Jarzębski to accompany her to a meeting with the music publisher, Michał Arct. Later that evening, in a letter to Andrzej, she described how the discussion went: 'I've just been to Arct's with old Jarzębski, but to be honest, I could have gone on my own, because he absolutely knows who I am. He is a nice young man who claims to be an ideological publisher. He treated me with great respect. I brought along my most recent piano and violin compositions, plus my *Children's Suite*; but he said straight away that he was interested in orchestral work. He doesn't pay for orchestral pieces, but it would be good if he printed them, wouldn't it? So, I've agreed to bring him the orchestral ones on Friday. I'll be interested to see what he picks. Of the ones I showed him today, he was most interested in the *Children's Suite*, because there might be a demand for that, but he asked me to leave all of them with him. They see sonatas and quartets as last in the queue, as they only shift a few copies a year of that kind of thing. He said that there's a real need for good-quality light music, not dance music, as after the war, none of the Germans is going to get played apart from Bach and Beethoven; but we don't have any light music. So, I'd really like to write a lovely operetta, but I have no idea how to find anyone for the libretto. Something like that would take off straight away. Our latest game with Alinka is carrying her around on our shoulders and on our heads.'[2]

Grażyna Bacewicz took the publisher's words seriously and set about composing a piece of light, popular music. She even met with success in this area, with one particular song. In her letters there is just a modest mention that this song has been sung on a number of occasions, and that the famous bass, Aleksander Michałowski, enjoys performing it.

On the fourth anniversary of the outbreak of World War II, BBC radio in London announced that heavy bombing raids were being carried out by the allied air force on Berlin. The increase in military operations was also being felt in Warsaw. Grażyna wrote to her husband: 'We have air-raid alarms every other day now. We don't wake Alinka up, but we're constantly on alert. There's just been the one time that we grabbed her and rushed down to the basement, when the explosions got really loud. We found out later that it had been anti-aircraft fire. In any case, the late hour of the alarm (of course) suggests that these are not visitors from the east, as previously.'

And then in October, before Andrzej was due to return, Grażyna wrote: 'The window glass has been fitted – our empty box of food supplies is now filled to the brim (we've bought twenty-odd kilos' worth plus a kilo of salt) – the rent's been paid, all the latest bills as well. They've damaged the electricity, I think on purpose, just so they can fix it. We're sitting with oil lamps and candles. It's hell. They've been collecting for repairs and they took 50 złotys off me. Anyway, about provisions. Bring some beans! It would be good to shell them now, straight away, so they dry out. I've only bought some peas, as I'm hoping you'll bring some beans. So: poppy seeds, beans and maybe a little wheat flour. Oh, and apples! (red ones)!'[2]

For Grażyna and other Varsovian musicians, the year 1943 ended with distressing news. In the early hours of 16 November 1943, the Gestapo arrested viola-player Henryk Trzonek, one of the musicians who had performed Grażyna's *String Quartet No. 2*. The Germans floodlit the town house where the Trzoneks' apartment was located, ran upstairs and stormed through the door. They beat up Henryk and then took him to Pawiak Prison. The Underground Musicians' Union tried to find a connection in some Gestapo unit. Funds were collected for the required bribe. Unfortunately, however, on 3 December 1943, the Germans publicly executed several prisoners; one of these was Henryk Trzonek.

Underground resistance

From the start of 1944, the Polish Underground began organizing an increasing number of operations, to which the Germans responded with cruel retaliatory measures. The desire to avenge the murder of Poles was growing.

The Bacewicz family spent Easter 1944 together in Maria's apartment on Mokotowska Street. Grażyna raced around the city to get hold of the things they needed. Andrzej treated patients, who in the afternoons used to gather in the waiting room of the apartment on Koszykowka Street. In the mornings, Grażyna answered the telephone, made appointments, and looked after their child, so by the evenings, she would be too tired to compose. Instead, as a form of relaxation, she wrote a short story. It arose imperceptibly, from scraps of conversations, absurd and often irritating ones that she exchanged with her husband's patients. She gave it the title: '*Czy to pan Doktor Potrowski*' ('Is that Dr Potrowski?')

In April, Andrzej left again for Marynin to continue his treatment for tuberculosis, which we learn from letters: '"Dear Daddy-kins! Please Daddy-kins, would you bring me a kitten, a croissant and an egg." That's what Alinka dictated I should write,' wrote Grażyna. 'We're worried that it's turned cold again, as it messes up your treatment. I'm asking you to please, please make sure you dress warmly and don't go out when it rains, and then keep the windows closed! Remember to do that! How are you feeling? Do you manage to get any fresh air? Be sure always to lie down for a while after dinner. I just don't like you wandering over to Lublin. If that's happened just the one time, then that's all right, but don't go doing any more trips of that kind. Woytowicz has offered me a performance with a singer on the twenty-sixth of May. I've agreed because it extends my permit. Alinka's healthy and happy.'[2]

Before Grażyna's performance as accompanist to the singer at Woytowicz's, Eugenia Umińska came down to Warsaw. She was no longer performing openly at public concerts, but she was happy to take part in underground ones. One such event took place on 3 May 1944 in Boduena Street in Stefan Wiśniewski's apartment. On that occasion she performed Szymanowski's concerto with the piano duo Lutosławski–Panufnik.

On 29 July 1944, a rumour went round that the Soviet armoured advance guard had reached the edge of the Praga district of Warsaw. Shooting could be heard on the other side of the River Vistula.

'Well, we'll soon be liberated,' Maria declared, putting on her hat.

'Where are you going, Mama?' asked Grażyna anxiously.

'I'm going back to Mokotowska Street. I have my plans!' she said, annoyed that her daughter was trying to control her.

'But Mama, there's a war going on. God knows what might happen at any moment. We should all stay together!'

'Together? But Kiejstut and Halszka haven't arrived yet.'

'They promised they'd come on Tuesday and stay the night.'

'So I'll come back then. I have to tidy my apartment and pop in to see the aunties.'

'Please stay, Mama; I have a bad feeling.'

'Wandzia will help you with Alinka,' Maria cut her off and, ignoring the sound of gunfire outside the window, walked out of the apartment. She met the caretaker in the courtyard, who was waving his broom around and saying how there were heavy German tanks from the Fallschirm-Panzer Division, 'Hermann Göring', going down Jerozolimskie Avenue, heading for the Praga district, and that the army was desperately trying to mine the Poniatowski and Kierbedzia bridges. His words did not convince the old lady, who, with a brisk step, passed through the gate and headed for Mokotowska Street.

Wanda turned out to be equally stubborn. Despite Grażyna's pleas, on the day the Warsaw Uprising broke out [1 August 1944], Wanda went off to work at the offices of the chemical plant 'Dobrolin'. On her way back, near Narutowicza Square, she boarded the number 11 tram, which shook and clattered its way to Politechniki Square. Suddenly shots rang out.

'You'd better run, Lady! It's "W" hour!' yelled the tram driver, and he grabbed his pistol and jumped off the tram.

Wanda too jumped out onto the road, bent down, and began running straight ahead. She arrived at some nearby allotments. There were a few people running alongside her. When they heard the bang of grenades, they dropped to the ground. A volley of machine-gun fire went flying above their heads. Wanda felt a hard knock against her legs. She tried to move, but she could not. She had been hit in the thigh, just above her knee. Her foot of the other leg had been shattered by bullets. A man leaned over her. His German speech was too fast for her to understand. He lifted her up as if she were as light as a feather and ran through the bullets towards the road. He laid her down alongside the wall of a house, and then he disappeared.

Medical personnel took Wanda to the nearest hospital, to the Sano Maternity Clinic on Lwowska Street, where Andrzej Biernacki (who had returned to Warsaw) was now working. As it turned out, Edmund Rudnicki was also in the building, in hiding, running an information programme on short-wave radio.

On 9 August 1944, a Polish Radio team, as a Government Delegation, started broadcasting a programme through the 'Błyskawica' ('Lightning') radio station on short wave, as well as on medium wave through a radio station that they had acquired. Information was being broadcast about the plight of the civilian population. Later, the radio also began warning people about the bad situation at the transit camp in Pruszków, which eventually alerted the Red Cross. Rudnicki ended up being not just a radio announcer, but also a performer; he was a proficient pianist. The Germans constantly targeted and shot at the radio station.

Wanda lay in hospital until 19 August. When things became dangerous, Andrzej arranged for the injured Wanda to be transported home to Koszykowa Street. Immobilized in her plaster armour, weak and in pain, she finally met up with her sister and mother. Grażyna described those days a year later, in a letter she wrote to her brother Vytautas, who was now living in the United States: 'We lived through more than two months of this hell. On the fifth day, Mummy walked through gunfire to reach our apartment, obviously not knowing anything about Wanda, who was suffering terribly and having to go through several operations. After 19 days, Wanda was brought to us from the hospital during the night, as everything around the hospital was going up in flames; so, we were together again later – the three of us and Alinka.

'After a month we couldn't live in the apartment any more, as the buildings around us were collapsing, so we carried Wanda down to the basement. I only went up to the apartment in order to cook something for them. We suffered terrible hunger. Alinka would cry for a small piece of bread, or a little potato. We ate ground barley. Mummy bore it quite well. Though usually a coward, I wasn't frightened during the Uprising. The bombs were the worst, the Big Berthas, the grenades (as we never knew when and where they might fall) and the so-called 'cow'. (You've probably not heard of that one.) All through the Uprising, Alinka dreamed that Uncle Witek from America would bring her a beautiful talking doll with eyes that opened and closed…

'We left Warsaw on 2 October and the Germans took us to the camp in Pruszków. Wandzia on a stretcher. Thanks to Wandzia we were put in the barracks for the sick, where they were setting people free. Those in the other barracks were being sent to do forced labour in Germany. So they let us go.

We went with Wandzia on her stretcher to the hospital in Grodzisk, and that's where we were.

'With the exception of my *Overture* (which I've recently reworked), I managed to rescue my compositions.'[2]

'Fate was on our side'

While still in hospital on Lwowska Street, Wanda sent a letter to Kiejstut and Halszka through the Scouts' field postal service. She reported on her condition and her two operations, as well as on their mother and Grażyna and Andrzej, who had taken in the Ekiers – a pianist and his wife, their young child and a mother-in-law. She said she was worried about Kiejstut and Halszka. The letter never reached the addressees; it was returned to Wanda 23 years later, in 1968. It turns out that the scout had not been able to carry out his task, since Grottgera Street, where Grażyna's brother and sister-in-law were living, had been under German fire. The occupants of the building had stuck together (like the inhabitants of Koszykowa Street) and had taken it in turn to do lookout shifts to warn each other of any danger. From time to time, insurgents would turn up in the courtyard, but no-one was ever able to oust the Germans from the area.

Following advice from the leader of an insurgent unit, Kiejstut and Halszka left their apartment. They met up with their family in Grodzisk Mazowiecki. How that came about is described by Grażyna in a letter written to Vytautas after the war: 'After the Uprising, Kiejstut and Halszka found out by complete chance about what had happened to Wandzia. At that point they still didn't know anything about us. Halszka was in some house in the countryside outside Warsaw, where, in exchange for food, she was looking after some children. A doctor came to the house and, by pure chance, unaware what relationship Halszka had to Andrzej and Wanda, he started telling her about him and Wanda. That's how they found out what had happened. They also found us by pure chance. They were meant to be going to Kraków to look for work, and they were passing through Milanówek, and that's where someone told them that Dr Biernacki was apparently in Grodzisk. So they arrived at Grodzisk, not remotely expecting to find us there. Can you imagine the joy – ours and theirs – when they walked in? We thought that they were doing forced labour in Germany.'[2]

In her letters to Vytautas, Grażyna described the tragedy of the destruction of war; 'Warsaw doesn't exist…there are no houses…no railway station, not a single bridge, or anything – nothing apart from piles of rubble. Don't think that I'm exaggerating. Whatever I write, it won't convey the extent of it… Mummy's house doesn't exist, burned down with Wandzia's beautiful library and everything. Kiejstut and Halszka have also lost everything. Our building's supposedly still standing (actually it's our annex that's still standing, because the other part of the building has collapsed), but we've been looted… But you know, Wituś, fate was on our side, and didn't want us to die. For example, Wanda, Kiejstut, and Andrzej were forever being caught up in 'round-ups', and they always somehow managed to wangle their way out. As our underground organization was carrying out operations, such as blowing up trains with the German army and killing some of the worst Gestapo officers, or stealing, say, carriages with ammunition, the Germans would punish us for it every day, or every few days, killing dozens of people on the streets of Warsaw in those very round-ups. You can imagine the state of agitation that we lived in, and how we were constantly afraid of everything. We even had a telephone installed at Mummy's, as after six o'clock we weren't allowed out, and during the night, God knows what might have happened, so we phoned each other constantly. During the worst times, we all gathered at ours, along with Kiejstut and Halszka, and we'd spend the night together, even though it was forbidden to stay overnight away from your own home.

'Throughout the entire war, I worried most, and constantly, about Wanda, because her place of work was a very long way from home, so the likelihood of disaster was greater. And the day that she got injured, she'd been staying overnight at our place, and we'd both dreamed of Chopin's funeral march. I begged her on bended knee not to go to the office, but she was determined to go. At some point we'll write and tell you about the delights of being in an air-raid. That was really fraying on the nerves as well. When the house next to mummy's got hit by a bomb and caught fire, they didn't know what to do, because sparks were flying into their rooms, and their place could have caught fire at any moment. Anyway, we were terribly lucky. No sooner had the Germans got a good kicking than Wandzia and I rushed out for work. We left for Lublin with mummy, Alinka, and Kiejstut.'[2]

'I've taken a fast pace'

From the letters that Grażyna wrote to her husband, we find that on 13 February 1945 she was still living in Lublin with her family. At the time she was trying to get work at the music school that was just being set up in Łódź. Andrzej stayed in Grodzisk, where he was running the Warsaw branch of the Dzieciątko Jezus (Infant Jesus) hospital. Grażyna wrote to him: 'So I'll be staying in Lublin for another six weeks or so. We'll be going to Marynin tomorrow for two days (we need a permit even for Marynin), and then we'll go back – me, Wanda, and Kiejstut, maybe even to our own place. Wanda is going to be working for *Gazeta Lubelska*, and Kiejstut and I have concerts. I've taken a fast pace, as Alinka's looking really raggedy. We're going to have to buy a lot of things.'[2]

Kiejstut and Grażyna gave concerts on the radio and public performances in February and March 1945, in the hall of the State Institute of Music, among other places. There was no shortage of repertoire. During the occupation, Grażyna had composed lots of new music. Dating from that period are her *Sonata* for solo violin, *Three Preludes for Piano*, *Piano Sonata No. 3* (later removed from her catalogue of works), *Suite for Two Violins*, *String Quartet No. 2*, as well as her *Overture for Orchestra*. She set to work energetically. To be able to perform without constraint, she took her little daughter to the village of Marynin and left her in the care of her mother and several aunts.

For her work in the editorial office of *Gazeta Lubelska*, Wanda received a basic salary of 80 złotys and was provided with lunch. She was paid extra for any text or articles she wrote. The joint budget ensured survival for the family during the difficult post-war period.

Grażyna and Kiejstut's concerts met with great success, as proven by the reviews from the first three performances.

After her last recital on 10 March 1945, Grażyna decided to leave for Łódź, to the Conservatoire, where she was taken on to teach both violin and music theory. She was expecting to receive an average salary, to be provided with meals, and most importantly, a furnished teacher's apartment. Obviously, she planned to give concerts. She dreamed of bringing her young daughter and her mother back to her as soon as possible. No doubt that was on her mind as she and Kiejstut made their way to Łódź in the 'county car', in other words, an ordinary lorry, covered with a heavy tarpaulin, that took a whole day to get there.

As soon as she reached her destination, she wrote to her husband: 'As regards the apartment, we arrived at quite a good time (not as good as those who got there first, who already have one, but still). That's because right now the business of getting a beautiful new building for the musicians is being sorted out. I was already on the list, and Kiejstut managed to get his name down as well. It looks as if I'll be having a lot of students, although I'm trying very hard not to, much to everyone's surprise, as the other teachers are just fighting to have as many as they can.'[2]

'I'm not just a professor; I'm a judge as well'

Students at the conservatoire in Łódź had heard about the lessons that Grażyna had given there ten years earlier, and droves of them signed up eagerly for her sessions. Kiejstut was also approached about giving piano lessons [as a secondary subject] and he too joined the teaching staff at the conservatoire.

The violinist and teacher, Irena Dubiska, performed at the opening of the conservatoire on 18 April 1945. On 22 April 1945 Grażyna and Kiejstut gave their first recital there, at a concert of chamber music: the inaugural event of the 'Conservatoire Concerts' cycle. They were to receive payment in kind for their performance. In Łódź they encountered lots of their old friends and acquaintances, including professors Antoni Dobkiewicz, Kazimierz Sikorski, Eugenia Umińska, and Tadeusz Sygietyński.

While she was waiting for allocation of her teacher's apartment, Grażyna stayed with Kiejstut and Halszka in a hotel at 26 Piotrkowska Street. Just as she had been as a student in Warsaw, she was cooped up in a tiny room. From her letters we learn that it was the lack of an apartment that bothered her the most: 'Dear Duduś!' she wrote to her husband. 'Were it not for the lack of apartment, I'd be feeling really good. I'm finally doing what I should be doing. What my salary's going to look like, and what his [Kiejstut's] salary's going to look like, we don't yet know. Not one of us, not even those who have been here a long time, has yet been given so much as an advance payment. We are in the Musicians' Union. At today's general meeting, I was selected to be on the peer jury, so watch out! I'm not just a professor; I'm a judge as well. *Voilà!*'[2]

In the end, the promised teacher's apartment fell through, but the teacher's salary amounted to 1500 złotys. Wanda was also able to contribute a fair amount of money to the family budget with the 1800 złotys she was earning as a journalist. Soon afterwards, they managed to bring Alinka and her grandmother over to Łódź. Meanwhile, Andrzej, who had had his title of 'Associate Professor' confirmed around June 1945, after National Victory Day was declared on 9 May at the end of World War II, visited his wife and daughter practically every weekend.

The fourth of June 1945 saw the Bacewicz siblings' second concert in Łódź, which Grażyna described in a letter to her husband: 'Well, Darling, it's all over now. Everything was wonderful beyond expectation. We're all so terribly sorry that you weren't there. Even though I was feeling very unwell, I played much better than I did at the other recital. We played brilliantly right from the start. The musicians absolutely loved it, and the audience shouted for an encore. I even had to go back to take a bow at the end of the first half. Górzyński kissed us, Raczkowski splashed out on some flowers, though mercifully he didn't present them to us on stage, and so on; it was just Irenka and Kazik Wiłkomirski who weren't there, as they're not here. The Palesters came, and they also absolutely loved it.'[2]

5 Compositions between Performances

It was going to be a busy autumn

In the summer of 1945, the conservatoire's administration team started preparations for reform, and the Intermediate School of Music was set up as a result. Kiejstut Bacewicz was appointed principal. The autumn was looking to be exceptionally busy, not just for Kiejstut, who was co-creating the core curriculum model for the future school, but also for Grażyna. The first of September 1945, saw the premiere of her *Overture* in Kraków as part of the first Festival of Polish Contemporary Music. It was performed by the Kraków Philharmonic Orchestra with Mieczysław Mierzejewski conducting. Grażyna had originally composed the *Overture* in 1943, but it had gone missing during the war, so she had rewritten the piece from scratch. We do not know, therefore, whether it sounds like her original composition.

By this time, Kraków was becoming the centre of the country's musical life. It was there that in April 1945 Tadeusz Ochlewski set up the Polish music publisher, Polskie Wydawnictwo Muzyczne (PWM). It was there too that the National Congress of Composers took place between 20 July and 2 September 1945, during which the Polish Composers' Union was formed.

By October 1945, Grażyna had around 16 concerts planned, of which two were symphonic ones, two were recitals and seven were radio appearances.

In September 1945, she wrote to Andrzej: 'I now have a few more concerts in October. After my recital in Kraków, I have a symphonic concert on the twelfth in Katowice (Karłowicz) and one in Bochnia on the fourteenth. After that Poznań and the area. I had this idea for a project today, that if I don't get an apartment in Łódź within the month (I'm making a last attempt, as I've got myself a letter from the Ministry, recommending me highly), then I'll give it all up in Łódź and we'll just move to Koszykowa Street. At least we'd be together. You'd have your little daughter with you, Mummy would have her beloved Warsaw, Wanda could have her operation, as her leg's really bothering her, and I'd write an operetta. In the worst case, I'd just have to travel up to Łódź for the day. This is just a rough plan.'[2]

The autumnal marathon tired Grażyna out to such an extent that she was 'running out of steam' (as she wrote to Andrzej). She and Kiejstut had travelled down to the festival in Kraków by train (from which all the windows had been removed) in a permanent draught. The concert, however, went brilliantly. The select audience added to the event – the cream of the literati, led by Julian Przyboś and Karol Kuryluk. They had to perform at least three encores. To the concert in Bochnia, Grażyna travelled by lorry, still dreaming all the while of a return to Warsaw, to the apartment in Koszykowa Street. She longed for a normal life, to be living with her family and her husband, without any lodgers.

In Kraków, the head of PWM, Tadeusz Ochlewski, agreed to publish a few of Grażyna's compositions, including her *Easy Duets on Folk Themes* for two violins, her *Concertino* and her *Easy Suite for Violin and Piano*. He also commissioned further pieces: compositions for violin with organ; pieces for small orchestra (with specified instrumentation), as well as folk pieces.

'But will I find the strength to do that?' wondered Grażyna, who was dying of exhaustion. In one letter, she wrote bitterly: 'I've had enough. I can't toil on like this. My darling little husband! Tell me, what am I supposed to do! I want to be ill. What I'd really like is for you to come up with some clever idea about me, something that would mean I could just have a little rest. I would be very, very grateful, Hubby darling! Really, I should just be sitting somewhere quietly in a corner, just composing and nothing else. This hassle with pupils is pointless, and the travelling to concerts is completely pointless as well… I love you so much.'[2]

At the start of December 1945, Grażyna gave yet another recital, this time in Katowice – the event passed agreeably – and when she eventually returned to Warsaw at the end of the year, she threw herself into composing with great gusto. The crowning achievement of this period is the *Concerto for String Orchestra*, which she wrote in 1948.

Paris, in a whirl of activity

In March 1946, Grażyna set off on a three-month-long tour of France. After six days of travelling by train, she arrived in Paris very tired, but full of optimism. Once again, she frequented her favourite little streets and breathed in the atmosphere of artistic freedom. This is what she had dreamed of during the war, while sheltering in the cellar. Yet Paris was no longer the same. Poverty was rife throughout the country, and people were hungry.

She stayed at the Ramzès hotel at 6 Rue des Moines. The first person she went to see as soon as she arrived was Monsieur Bouchoné, who was regarded as the greatest impresario in Paris. He listened intently to her playing, was delighted by it, and immediately set about organizing concerts for her. On 9 May 1946, Grażyna performed at the Salle Pleyel, playing Karol Szymanowski's *Violin Concerto No. 1* with the Orchestre Lamoureux, under the baton of the famous conductor Paul Kletzki. On 23 May 1946 she gave a recital at the Salle Gaveau where, together with the pianist Jerzy Witas, she played her *Sonata da Camera*, as well as pieces by Niccolò Paganini, Gaetano Pugnani, Antoni Szałowski, Henryk Wieniawski, Manuel de Falla, Lili Boulanger, and Ernst von Dohnányi. The proceeds of this concert, organized by the Association of Polish Women, went to Polish children affected by war. She was unable to practise in the hotel, so she prepared for her concerts at the homes of her friends, who would leave her the keys to their apartments.

In a letter to Vytautas, she wrote: 'On 27 April, there's a concert of chamber music in Salle Gaveau, where I'll be playing my *Suite for Two Violins*, and before that I also have a recital mainly for the Polish community, and in May a really big recital in Lyon. Oh yes – I'm also playing at the Sorbonne, as they're interested in Slavonic music in general, so they asked me if I'd agree to play. I wrote to you earlier from Warsaw, asking you to send me some strings from America. Did you get that letter? I'm renewing my request, as there aren't any decent strings in Europe. If you can, of course, I'd be very grateful.'[2]

Grażyna's performances caught the attention of the French critics. Excellent reviews appeared in *Parisian Weekly*, *France au Combat*, *Courrier de Paris*, *Opéra*, *Résistance*, and *Images Musicales*. She was praised for her virtuoso technique and her understanding of different styles. Reviewers wrote that through her combined skills as a composer and a performer, her interpretations brilliantly conveyed the essence of each piece.

Grażyna found herself caught up in a whirl of activity. Her career took off exponentially. She returned briefly to Poland to perform Mendelssohn's *Violin Concerto in E Minor*; and on 18 October 1946 she gave the premiere of her *Concerto No. 2 for Violin and Orchestra* with the Łódź Philharmonic Orchestra, with Tomasz Kiesewetter conducting. In 1947 she was back giving concerts in Paris. At the École Normale de Musique, she performed her *Sonata No. 2 for Violin and Piano* with the pianist Jean Germain, and pieces by Vivaldi, Bach, Szymanowski, Ravel, Poulenc, Stravinsky, and Mussorgsky, as well as her own transcription of Paganini's *Caprice No. 24*.

Structural rules

In June 1947, *Ruch Muzyczny* (*Musical Movement*) published an interview with Grażyna Bacewicz. The focus of the conversation was French music, but the following questions came up at the end:

'Did you play any Polish music?'

'Yes. Szymanowski's *Nocturne and Tarantella* and my own *Sonata No. 2*, which appealed to the French, though I don't like it myself.'

'Did you compose during your stay in Paris?'
'Of course. I wrote *Quartet No. 3*, which I'm proud of. Paris has something that's difficult to put into words, but that's conducive to creative work.'[8]

That must indeed have been the case, as the melodic line in the *Andante* movement of *Quartet No. 3*, which Bacewicz wrote while in Paris, has a seductive beauty to it, while the entire piece has a Mozartian logic. For Grażyna Bacewicz, the musical structure of a piece always came first.

'I tend to walk alone, as my main concern in my compositions is form,' she wrote to her brother, Vytautas. 'I work on the assumption that, if you arrange things higgledy-piggledy, or throw stones onto a pile, you'll never get a building out of it, and that kind of pile will always collapse. So too, in a musical work, you have to have structural rules, which will allow the work to stand on its own two feet. Obviously, these rules don't necessarily have to be ancient ones – God forbid. The music can be simpler or more complex (it doesn't matter; that's down to the language of the individual composer) but what it does need to be, in my opinion, is well constructed. I'm not even talking about good orchestration, because that's a given. I've rejected my old compositions. Now that I know more than I used to, I can see big faults in these compositions. Why then should they exist?'[2]

To be able to compose in peace, without the constant interruptions of performance, became her dream. Although she had met with huge success, she was feeling very tired. She felt overwhelmed by her career as a virtuoso. She confided in her brother: 'If someone told me that I had to give up my career as a violinist, I'd be only too delighted. I play, because it doesn't behove me to stop, through force of habit, oh, and that's how in Poland I earn a living; but I'd prefer to earn less, to have some peace, and to sit at home and compose. That's what I dream of. I travel around Poland giving concerts, but I only compose in passing, by night. It's not right.'[2]

Fortunately, Grażyna Bacewicz was possessed of the unusual gift of being able to do everything at considerably greater speed than other people. This applied as much to domestic matters as it did to musical ones. She was as capable of cooking dinner for the whole family within the space of an hour (where others would have spent half a day preparing in the kitchen) as she was of writing a major composition within the space of two weeks. The slowness of those around her often irritated her. Professor Sikorski, who had known her since her schooldays, was very well aware of this. On meeting with his pupil, he would ask her good-naturedly: 'Well, now, Grażynko, tell me – how many symphonies have you written today?'

This was not merely an innocent jokey comment from an elderly teacher, as between 1945 and 1947, among other compositions, Grażyna Bacewicz wrote her *Symphony No. 1*, *Violin Concerto No. 2*, *Introduction and Capriccio* for symphony orchestra, two sonatas for violin and piano, *String Quartet No. 3*, as well as many educational and popular pieces, in line with the Government's cultural policy which, initially, did not interfere with artists' intentions.

Grażyna spent July 1947 with her family in Szklarska Poręba, in the villa Muza on Słowackiego Street. There they met up with Kazimierz Sikorski's family. But even then, Grażyna Bacewicz did not waste any time; she worked on the proofs of her *Symphony No. 2*.

On returning to Warsaw, she performed at a concert in November, led by the English conductor, Clarence Raybould. She had made herself a long, white dress specially for the occasion, and she even changed her hairstyle. She put her hair up at the back and curled it at the front with three big rollers, so that it covered most of her forehead. She looked stunning. For her encore she played Dohnányi, Chopin, Wieniawski, and Albéniz, while the astonished conductor (unused to the custom of playing an encore) sat on stage, listening and applauding. Before the concert, Benedykt Dorys himself took a press photo and a beautiful portrait photo, which was to be hung in the Philharmonic. Clearly, most of the audience had come just to hear Grażyna Bacewicz, as the second half of the concert was less well attended.

Olympic Cantata

The year 1948 was an important one in the professional career of Professor Andrzej Biernacki. He took up the position of Director of the Clinic of Internal Diseases at the Medical University of Warsaw. In 1951 he would become a member of the Polish Academy of Arts and Sciences.

Grażyna also spent the year 1948 working intensively. In a letter to Andrzej, who was then on a work trip in Prague, she wrote (amongst other things) about a concert on 15 February, when she and Kiejstut had performed the premiere of her *Sonata No. 3 for Violin and Piano*; about her radio performance on 19 February with the *Sonata No. 2*; about plans for a trip to Kraków to perform her *Trio* and her songs; about the plenary assembly of the Polish Composers' Union; and also about 'writing for the Olympics' – a piece for a competition organized by the Polish Composers' Union. This last was her *Olympic Cantata*, set to an ode by Pindar. Grażyna won second prize for this composition in Poland and a commendation at the International Olympic Art Competition in London. (The gold medal was won by Zbigniew Turski for his *Olympic Symphony*.)

That summer in Zakopane, the weather was bad; the rain fell steadily against the windowsills. Grażyna grabbed a piece of paper and began writing to her husband: 'Dear Andrzej, We've just read in the paper that I and a few others have been given commendations in London. I've just received a congratulatory telegram from the Union. Just in case, I want to tell you where my passport is. So, I think it's in the bag that's hanging on the chair in the dining room, and if not, then it's somewhere on my shelves, and if not there, then as a last resort, try the right-hand drawer of the dresser. Does the Ministry expect the six people who were commended to go out there, or not? If yes (though I'm not desperate to go), then you'd have to take my passport to the International Relations Office, or to the Ministry. You'd have to hand it in personally; don't rely on anyone else. I won't bother you with anything else. So, do find out what you can, and write and let me know straight away! If Iwaszkiewicz and others go, I'll go as well; if not, then obviously I'm not keen.'[2]

The trip did not materialize in the end.

The honour of Polish composers restored by a 'gal'

In 1948 Grażyna finished writing her *Concerto for String Orchestra*, which brought her fame. It turned out to be her crowning compositional achievement from that period. It was written with a tripartite structure (*Allegro; Andante; Vivo*) and her characteristic compositional technique of combining Baroque *concerto grosso* style with classical style in the same piece. Its vigorous main theme, based on pendulum motion, has essentially become her creative trademark.

The piece's premiere was given by WOSPR (Polish National Radio Symphony Orchestra) with Grzegorz Fitelberg conducting, on 18 June 1950, during a General Meeting of the Polish Composers' Union in Warsaw.

One can well imagine how excited Grażyna's family must have been to read Stefan Kisielewski's review in *Tygodnik Powszechny* (*The General Weekly*): 'I can honestly say that, on this occasion, the honour of Polish composers was restored by a "gal", Grażyna Bacewicz. Her *Concerto for String Orchestra*, written with energy and panache, full of flowing inventiveness and excellent ideas on instrumentation, finally roused us from our lethargy. The piece harks back to Bach or Handel – a kind of contemporary Brandenburg Concerto. We finally got our teeth into a "rare piece" of wholesome and tasty music, written with creative power – a truly virile one.'[13]

The year 1948 also saw the creation of Grażyna's *Violin Concerto No. 3*. This is how she wrote about it in her private notebook: 'It is based on the folk music of the Podhale region, from which, as well as the mood, I have tried to take characteristic melodic phrases, harmonic combinations, and rhythmic features. In the first part, none of the themes is based on Góral (Highlander) songs, as opposed to the second part, in which both themes (I say both because it's in sonata form) are based on folk songs. They've been reworked, obviously. The first theme of the second part is based on a little-known tune, a very beautiful one. In the third part, only one of the secondary themes (the slow one) gets picked up again...'[8]

A somewhat longer note describes in detail the construction of the piece, a rare departure for the composer, given her steely resolve not to disclose the secrets of her compositional technique. She probably made the notes in preparation for a public statement. Her *Violin Concerto No. 3* had its premiere on 4 March 1949 at the Baltic Philharmonic, with Stefan Śledziński conducting and the composer as soloist. In July 1949 Grażyna performed it in Ukraine while on a tour of the country with a group of Polish musicians.

A bouquet of roses from the embassy

In May 1948, an International Congress of Composers and Music Critics took place in Prague. The conclusions drawn at the time did not fill people with optimism. It became clear that the musical world was now also being affected by the tenets of socialist realism that were already in force within the Soviet Union. A musical festival was also held during the Congress. Witold Lutosławski's *Symphony No. 1* and Grażyna Bacewicz's *Overture* were performed, among other pieces. Grażyna's *Overture* was conducted by Zdzisław Górzyński. On the evening of 18 May 1945, Grażyna wrote to her husband from Prague: 'There were a lot of people at the concert. The *Overture* went down well; and, of course, once the audience saw that it was a young woman (I was wearing a long gown), they became even more enthusiastic. I went up to Górzyński from below stage, and he handed me a bouquet of roses from the embassy. Later we went to a reception at the embassy itself. There were 500 people there. Can you imagine the crowds? But I felt at ease, and I met lots of people. Ekier* and I had a drink and we're now on first-name terms.'[2]

That same day Grażyna also sent a letter to New York, to Vytautas, who had been living in America since World War II. He had been trying, unsuccessfully, to obtain American citizenship, as he had turned down a passport from the Soviet Union and was consequently a stateless person. 'Dear Brother! I am in Prague at a Contemporary Music Festival. Today they played my *Overture*. It went down brilliantly. Tomorrow I'm playing on the radio. I'm taking the opportunity to write to you from a foreign country, and I'm asking you, Vitusiu Dearest, to never say anything daft in your letters, so we don't end up in gaol. Please do not write any more about communists and photos, or about our trips to America etc. All your letters are censored in Poznań. They're opened because they've supposedly been poorly stuck down. Lots of love, Grażyna.'[2]

---

*   Translator's note: Jan Ekier (1913–2014) was a renowned pianist, piano teacher, and composer.

6 Art versus Realism

Conference in Łagów

In 1949 Grażyna Bacewicz was awarded the City of Warsaw Prize.

This year made it into the music history books on account of the Conference of Composers and Music Critics, which took place from 5 to 8 August in Łagów Lubuski. The period of darkest Stalinism and ideological pressure was just beginning. The gathering in Łagów was meant to create the illusion of a meeting of ideas and dialogue between creative minds and those in authority. The Deputy Minister for Culture and Arts, Włodzimierz Sokorski, took part in the discussion, along with the composers' representative, the Marxist musicologist Zofia Lissa. The then president of the Polish Composers' Union, Zygmunt Mycielski, along with Sokorski, delivered the keynote lectures. In the summary discussion, formalism in art was clearly presented as being in opposition to realism. 'But in music can one really talk about realism?' thundered Sokorski from the podium, while the audience members, exhausted after many hours of sitting, slumped in their seats. The words sounded imperious and overpowering:

'So, realism in music should not be treated mechanically, not as a new artistic school, as in these circumstances we would be taking the very essence of realism in art to the point of absurdity. Rather we should treat it as a conscious relationship to our own musical creativity, as being the creative outcome of society's specific needs, expressed in a specific musical language, its principles based on those of the great classics in theme, tonality, harmony of musical language, on its folk character and national style.'[8]

After three days of endless discussions under the watchful eye of the portrait of Stalin, which seemed to judge the speakers harshly, it was established that the cosmopolitanism of rotten, decadent bourgeois art had to be opposed through a robust national art. The Marxist aesthetic, however, laid down unity of form and content. It was stipulated that vocal-instrumental pieces be written, rather than 'formalistic' instrumental music. The dark period of pseudo-artistic shows organized by groups of labourers or rural workers on a monumental scale had just begun. Dust generated by the foot-tapping of thousands of feet began flying off community centre floorboards and theatre stages. Theatrical performances turned into huge all-singing and all-dancing spectacles, intended to depict the life and struggle of the nation and all the working people in the towns and villages. In a word, art was to become classless and populist and embrace the masses with its wide-spread red wings.

Zofia Lissa and Józef Chomiński coined the concept of creating an art that came from the people and would be returned to the people in a richer form.

Piano Concerto

Grażyna, like other composers, had to somehow survive the period of Stalinism. Years later, in a eulogy dedicated to Artur Malawski, Grażyna recalled just how much Polish musicians were bothered by the burden of pressure and restrictions at the time, and what lovely memories of Parisian creative freedom and hope were brought to her while listening to Maławski's *Trio*.

She did not enter the 1949 competition to compose a piece of music for mass singing, in which Witold Lutosławski won second prize. She did not write a cantata about Stalin or any revolutionary song, as did Tadeusz Baird. One way out of this situation was to draw on folk music. This is what Grażyna did when she wrote her *Piano Concerto*, combining folk themes with textural tension and virtuosity. Using a full orchestral line-up, she built up powerful climaxes. The solo piano part is brilliant and showy. Grażyna composed this piece especially for the Fryderyk Chopin Composers' Competition organized by the Polish Composers' Union to mark the hundredth anniversary of the composer's death. She was awarded second prize. (No first prize was awarded.)

In the second, autumnal, edition of this competition, Grażyna was awarded further prizes. She received a commendation for her *Étude* and third prize for her *Concert Krakowiak*, a piece that she had dedicated to the pianist Stanisław Szpinalski, who gave its first performance. Szpinalski also premiered Grażyna's *Piano Concerto* (on 4 November 1949) with the Warsaw Philharmonic Orchestra, conducted by Andrzej Panufnik.

Grażyna Bacewicz's most significant piece from the year 1949 is, however, the *Sonata No. 4 for Violin and Piano*, dedicated to her brother Kiejstut. This is a deep composition that reaches into the realms of transcendental music. It is one of Grażyna's most mature pieces, and combines drama, pathos, lyricism, and playfulness. It is in four parts. After an introduction, the first part opens with a lively two-themed *Moderato*, its second theme referring to a lyrical folk song. The lyrical *Andante ma non troppo* is followed by a grotesque *Scherzo*, and the whole piece is rounded off with a solemn *Finale*.

On 26 September 1950 in Kraków, Grażyna gave her first public performance of this sonata with her brother Kiejstut. They performed in the hall of the music publisher Polskie Wydawnictwo Muzyczne (PWM). For this piece, the composer was awarded first prize at the inaugural Festival of Polish Music in Warsaw in 1951.

'No nerves whatsoever'

From the creative point of view, 1950 was not as dynamic for Grażyna as previous years had been. Every composer, however prolific, sometimes stops to catch her breath. Grażyna began the year with a tour of Romania, where she performed her *Violin Concerto No. 3*. That autumn she gave nine recitals in Czechoslovakia with the pianist Alfred Holeček (in Třinec, Brno, České Budějovice, Prague, Žilina, and Bratislava).

After her first concert, she wrote to her family: 'It took place at the Opera – a very large hall. It all went unexpectedly well. There were lots of people; we played well and it went down very well indeed. At the end of the first half (after *Sonata No. 4*) I had to go out and take a bow five times. Loads of encores. I played without any nerves whatsoever. Everyone was happy – the people, me, the consul, although he doesn't know anything, and so on. There was a reception at my hotel later. My room's full of flowers. Tomorrow Żuławski is coming here, and we're supposed to be travelling to Cieszyn for the premiere of Kruczkowski's *The Germans*. I'll give him an earful, and apart from that I'll discuss various things with him. It's good that the first concert isn't in Prague, as the pianist will have time to polish the *Sonata*. We'll not be playing *Sonata No. 4* in Třinec, because the audience there is mostly working-class, but we will be in Brno. I played in my taffeta dress. I'll go to Třinec in my red one, as I don't want to risk spoiling the taffeta. If it weren't for the fact that I'm ill, everything would be fine! So, goodnight for now. I'll finish off tomorrow. Bye! I keep playing patience to see if all's well with you. It's funny that I've suddenly become a violinist. I'll be travelling the length and breadth of Bohemia.'[2]

For her last concert away from home in 1950, Grażyna travelled to Budapest, where she performed her *Violin Concerto No. 3* yet again, this time with Grzegorz Fitelberg conducting the Budapest Radio Orchestra.

Before the end of the year, which the family spent in Zakopane, she started work on her *Symphony No. 2*, which she dedicated to the conductor Witold Rowicki. The symphony was premiered the following year at the inaugural Festival of Polish Music.

String Quartet No. 4

The year 1951 brought with it world fame for Grażyna, as her *String Quartet No. 4* won first prize at the International String Quartet Competition in Liège. The *Quartet*, as Grażyna explained in an interview to *Kurier Codzienny* (*The Daily Courier*) on 10 October 1951, consists of three movements and makes the most of each of the instruments, while the melodies have recurring 'folk themes'.

At that point, Grażyna's mother, Maria Modlińska, sat down by lamplight and opened up her small grid-paper notebook, which she had carefully covered with brown paper. In her practised, calligraphic hand, worthy of a graduate of an institution for well-bred young ladies, she described this event in detail. From this moment onwards, the notes in Maria's little notebook become inseparable companions to the life and career of her busy daughter.

'11 December 1951, Warsaw, Tuesday. Oh joy! Beautiful weather for Grażyna's return from Belgium. I waited at home with afternoon tea. The table laid, the apartment full of flowers. The plane had a two-hour delay. They arrived home after 6 p.m. Though very tired and looking slimmer, Grażyna was in excellent mood. She was carrying a massive bunch of gorgeous pink and white carnations with ribbons in those same colours and an enormous box in the shape of a couch, covered in colourful silk, with fabulous Belgian chocolates from the embassy in Brussels. Grażyna began telling us about her travels, from when she left for Belgium to her return today. About her concerts in the embassy in Belgium, the four in Liège and other cities. She did a radio recording. She had eight concerts in all. Everywhere she met with great success and, on the eighth of the month, she had an awards ceremony – prizes and degrees. Grażyna's degree certificate is still there [in Belgium], awaiting signature. In the first half of all the concerts, the Quatour Municipal de Liège played Grażyna's *String Quartet No. 4*, which had won first prize at the International String Quartet Competition in the city. And in the second half Grażyna played her own *Sonata No. 4* with the excellent local pianist Monique Pichon. Grażyna had a huge amount of work to do during her two-week stay, but got so much satisfaction out of it. They gave her an exceptionally warm and enthusiastic welcome, were very lovely and hospitable towards her and took a great interest in her compositions. They're going to be playing them.'[1]

Grażyna brought back lots of presents with her from Belgium for family and friends. In her notebook, Maria excitedly lists things that, at the time, could not be obtained in Polish shops: 'Mandarins, lemons, confectionery, bananas. And for a whole range of different colleagues, friends and acquaintances, lots of cosmetics, a whole load of different vitamins, medicines, strings, sheet music, chocolate, cigarettes, perfume, nylons, a machine for sharpening razors and many, many other items. She spent all her prize money and all the fees from her concerts in Liège; and she also contributed some money to artistic causes in Belgium.'[1]

From Maria's earlier notes we get the inside story of how the *String Quartet No. 4* came into being: 'On 10 May 1951, with quite a few different compositions at development stage, Grażyna decided to write a composition for a competition recently announced in Liège: her *String Quartet No. 4*. Despite having various jobs to do at home, extensive correspondence and meetings with the Polish Composers' Union (ZKP), with the music publisher PWM, having to be a competition juror, trying to get the home guest-ready for the holidays, on 31 May 1951 Grażyna finished her [*String*] *Quartet No. 4* and sent it off to PWM, for them to transcribe; but on account of the very tight deadline, PWM returned the *Quartet*, and Grażyna then gave it to a music copyist at the ZKP, who sat on it for a long time. On 12 June, the copyist brought the *Quartet* back in such a poor state of transcription that Grażyna wept over it and had to spend many hours correcting and pasting, wearing herself out and working at high speed to get it posted to Liège in time to meet the deadline. And sure enough, two quartets from Poland, Grażyna Bacewicz's and Zbigniew Turski's, posted by the ZKP, did indeed arrive in Liège with two minutes to spare before the competition deadline. On 5 October 1951 Grażyna received a phone call from PAP [Polish Press Agency] informing her that she was the winner. This extremely joyful piece of news took her completely by surprise and she just stood there all red-faced, and we were completely stunned. Such a huge success, just the happiest of days, so that we all started jumping about like mad things and hugging and kissing one another. Our brilliant little lady (as we were soon told) had beaten 54 men from 13 different countries.'[1]

On her return to Poland, Grażyna Bacewicz's life changed dramatically. She gave countless interviews, posed for photographs, talked about the success she had had with her concerts. When asked about her plans for the future, she said that she was currently working on her *Symphony No. 3*, that she wanted to write a second piano sonata and a fifth violin concerto, as well as smaller works for the violin. In addition to photographers, she had artists coming to her apartment to draw her portrait. Her home had never been so lively, and all the minor matters there were overseen by Grażyna's mother, Maria: tiny in size, but strong in spirit.

A year later, at the end of September and beginning of October 1952, Grażyna was in Belgium once again – as a member of the jury for the International String Quartet Competition in Liège, where her *String Quartet No. 4* was one of the set pieces.

Her trips to Belgium allowed Grażyna to distance herself from things that were taking place in her home country. During her first visit to Belgium, she sent a letter to America. She knew that there would be no censorship, which there frequently was in the case of correspondence sent from or received in Poland.

'Dear Witek, I'm taking advantage of being in a territory where I can write honestly. Please understand, my Dear Brother, that we are prisoners and that we might, at any moment for the slightest thing, be sent to prison. We are managing well financially, as I'm earning a lot. Of course, there are many things that we can't get hold of here, e.g. meat, ham (we get a little bit with ration coupons every ten days), not to mention chocolate or things like that. But we're not suffering in material terms. In terms of spirit, however, it's just desperate. We often say that it's a good thing that you're not in Lithuania, or with us, because you wouldn't have been able to stand it. We're also desperately sorry for Father, because he'll certainly have it worse than we do, and he's on his own at that.'[2]

She writes her next letter to him on her return to Warsaw, this time softening her tone: 'It seems I misinformed you about our commissioning process. It's a wonderful thing, and the envy of the whole of Western Europe. We get dosh from the state, so that we can work in peace. Did Bach write so much as one piece that hadn't been commissioned? And I'd rather get it from the state than from a particular individual. Don't think that all we write is pieces for mass choral singing. I get commissions for quartets, symphonies, concertos, as well as educational pieces. Maybe there are certain trends in the commissions, let's say a greater number of operas and cantatas that are accessible to everyone, but essentially, everyone does what they know how to do.'[2]

On the very day that the Quatuor Municipal de Liège was playing Grażyna Bacewicz's *Quartet No. 4* – on 21 September 1951 – Warsaw saw the premiere of her *Cello Concerto No. 1*. This piece had been commissioned by the cellist Miloš Sádlo, who performed it with the Warsaw Philharmonic Orchestra, with Witold Krzemieński conducting during the inaugural Festival of Polish Music. The *Concerto* adheres to classical principles: there are contrasts between the three movements. The first movement is in sonata-allegro form and the third in sonata-rondo form. The composer does, however, express herself in her own individual language.

Composing regardless of everything

Before her trip to Belgium, Grażyna was already writing her *Violin Concerto No. 4*. It seems that with the increasing frenzy around her (arrangements for future concerts, various meetings with the ZKP Polish Composers' Union, negotiations with her publisher PWM, looking after her daughter who was frequently ill, possibly due to the war-time conditions of food scarcity at the time of her birth), it was only by a miracle that she managed to find a quiet moment for composing. Entries of the following kind make a rare appearance in Maria's diary: '4 November, Sunday… A happy little day for Grażyna, as she's had no interruptions from anyone while composing her *Violin Concerto No. 4*. Such a very rare day.' [1]

ART VERSUS REALISM   **65**

The composer finally completed the piece once her 'ladies' had gone skiing in Zakopane, which Maria, as usual, noted diligently: 'Oh joy! A telegram from Grażyna to say that she'll be arriving tomorrow morning. Then a little letter. She says she'll be bringing caricatures of the four prize-winning composers in Liège, printed in the programme sent by Poulet. Very funny. But, most importantly, on 31 December 1951 she finished her *Violin Concerto No. 4*. Then in a great hurry she wrote out the violin part and the instrumental parts of the three movements of the concerto. In the new year, Grażyna entertained her colleagues: the Lutosławskis, the Rowickis, the Panufniks, Gradstein and his lady, Count Mycielski, Szeligowski, Lissa, and Żuławski. They partied until late – had a great time.'[1]

Grażyna Bacewicz's *Violin Concerto No. 4* had its premiere on 21 February 1952 in Kraków (hence the great hurry to write out and transcribe the orchestral parts). The solo part was played by the composer herself, with the Kraków Philharmonic Orchestra accompanying her, and Bohdan Wodiczko conducting.

Symphony No. 3

Symphony No. 3, which had been commissioned by the Ministry of Culture and Art, was finished by Grażyna on 28 June 1952. It was a Saturday, and, outside, the sun was shining. Maria and her granddaughter Alinka were out walking in Ujazdowski Park when Grażyna wrote her final note on the stave. She had been in a great hurry to get the commission finished on time. A week earlier, Maria had noted: 'Grażyna has told PWM that she's finished her *Symphony No. 3*. The score is with PWM. They're getting the orchestral parts written out. The premiere is September in Kraków with Wodiczko. She's asked for a letter to be sent to the Ministry…about her second instalment for this symphony. And to let PWM know that she'll get the fourth movement of the symphony over to them in a week's time. Length of piece: approx. ½ hour.'[1]

Symphony No. 3 was performed according to plan on 11 September 1952. Grażyna attended the premiere. A feature of this symphony is its monothematic nature. The piece opens with a powerful, uplifting introduction: *Drammatico*. Comparisons may be drawn with the opening of Brahms's *Symphony No. 1 in C Minor*; however, the harmony in Bacewicz's *Symphony No. 3* is clearly rooted in the twentieth century.

Professor Sikorski would not have been surprised by Grażyna's tempo of work. Nor would Grzegorz Fitelberg, who was trying to persuade Grażyna to compose her next symphony especially for him, which Grażyna agreed to do.

'I must hurry'

In the middle of July 1952, the entire family, apart from Andrzej, left for the countryside. They stayed on a farm in the village of Koszelówka, near Gąbin, occupying part of a wooden country cottage, with a shady veranda that led out onto a smallish garden. They were surrounded by the sound of rustling forests and the sight of storks wandering over the fields and meadows, while across the road, among the trees, they could see the shimmering surface of Lake Zdworskie. Maria did not idle her time away. Even while on holiday, she wrote in her journal: 'It worries me that Grażyna is getting back to work in August. She'll only have had a short rest after such an intense year of creative work. She keeps saying: "I have to leave a lot behind me – I must hurry." She'll be leaving in a few days' time to compose her *Piano Quintet*. Let's hope no-one disturbs her.'[1]

Grażyna wrote on the move, often after concerts, or at night-time. She worked quickly and constantly, as if in a race against time, which, she sensed (and she had already written about this feeling in her courtship letters to Andrzej) she had little left.

In the first half of the 1950s, Grażyna Bacewicz composed three symphonies (*Nos. 2, 3, and 4*), her *Violin Concerto No. 4*, *Piano Quintet No. 1*, *Oberek No. 2* for violin and piano, *Piano Sonata No. 2*, *The Polish Overture* for orchestra, *Violin Concerto No. 5*, *Partita* in different versions (for violin and piano and also for orchestra), *Sonatina* for piano, *Sonatina* for oboe and piano, *String Quartet No. 5*, and many other pieces.

On 2 August 1952, Grażyna boarded the bus in Gąbin and returned to Warsaw. It was quiet in the apartment on Koszykowsa Street. Andrzej had gone to Łeba for whole of the month of August. She was able to compose her *Piano Quintet No. 1* in peace. She gave the piece four movements. She made full use of the tonal possibilities of each instrument, introduced virtuosic elements and references to folk tunes.

The piece was premiered a few months later, on 16 November 1952, by the Kraków Quartet with Kiejstut on the piano. It is regarded as an excellent composition, deeply personal emotionally, logically-constructed, and written with passion.

In far-off Lithuania

On 22 September 1952, news reached Warsaw concerning Vincas Bacevičius's worsening state of health. 'Sad news about Daddy,' wrote a worried Maria. 'He's ill with his intestines, all skin and bones. He weighs 62 kg; he used to weigh ninety-odd.'[1]

The following month, Maria and Wanda sat down to write a letter to Kaunas.

'Write to your father about Grażynka's most recent successes,' said Maria. 'I'm sure that'll make him happy. That they're playing her *Quartet No. 4* in France, Holland, Italy, Spain, Austria, the GDR, even in America. That in the middle of November, her *Piano Quintet No.1* and her *Sonata No. 5* are going to be premiered in Kraków with Kiejstut, and that she'll be playing her *Violin Concerto No. 4* on the coast. That Grażyna's been asked to be on the jury at the Wieniawski Competition in Poznań in December. That her *Cello Concerto No. 1* has been sent to Kraków to Zofia Adamska, who's going to be playing it in November.'

When she had finished writing the letter, Wanda put it in her handbag and, despite the rain, ran out to the post office. When she got back, she sat down to work, and so the apartment was filled with the tip-tapping of her typewriter. Maria started clearing up in the kitchen; and then she put Alinka to bed, as that evening, Grażyna had gone to a meeting at the Ekiers', at which Lutosławski, Żuławski, Rudnicki, and Panufnik were also present.

Vincas Bacevičius never recovered from his serious illness. On 17 January 1953 the family received a letter (sent from Kaunas on 2 December of the previous year) in which relatives informed them that if they wanted to say goodbye to their father, they would have to come to Lithuania straight away.

What were they to do in that situation? To be granted permission from senior officials for a trip to the Soviet Socialist Republic of Lithuania, one first had to make an application and then wait ages for a decision, and in any case, a positive outcome was not guaranteed. It may be assumed that it was no accident that the letter had been delayed, and that the censorship office deliberately held onto it. In those days not a single letter would have slipped past the sticky fingers of the secret police. The news that their father was in such a bad way came as a shock to everyone. Beset by uncertainty, they sent a telegram to Kaunas and awaited a reply.

On 18 January 1953, a telegram arrived from Kaunas: 'Father died 22 December 1952. Buried in Višako Ruda, under the oak tree next to Piotr – his brother, who died a week earlier.'[1]

Maria well remembered the moment when her husband and his brother planted the oak tree on the grave of their own father in 1905. Forty-seven years had passed since that time, of which only eighteen had been spent with her husband. For the remaining 29 years, they had lived apart from each other. The family was scattered, but its members had always remained exceptionally close to each other spiritually.

On the Jury of the Wieniawski Competition

In December 1952, before the painful news reached Warsaw, Grażyna had left for a two-week-long trip to Poznań in her capacity as member of the jury of the Second Henryk Wieniawski Violin Competition. During that time, she wrote and rang home frequently, even sent telegrams.

'My Golden Ones, my Dears – my Wee Alineczko! There's a young French lady playing right now. She's playing rather well, and the audience is crazy about her. The audience has warmed up so much that even after the *Polish*

Caprice, they started calling out, "Composer!", which they've never done before after the *Oberek*. Obviously, I kept quiet. I haven't told you yet that we've been sitting at a long table in the hall, in front of the rows of seats (lots of rows have been taken out).

'Jarzębski's been causing havoc unintentionally. He moved Jahnke's chair. Jahnke didn't realize, and he fell over, bringing Jarzębski down with him, and the two of them fell over, legs in the air, onto the flowers which separate our table from the audience. Then the Bulgarian who was sitting next to me got a terrible fright, because he thought that Jarzębski was dying. I forgot to bring my music with me from home, and now I'm going to have to buy some, because the foreigners want it.'[2]

Grażyna returned to her hotel in the early hours of 10 December 1952. The deliberations following the first round of the competition had just finished. She didn't feel like going to sleep yet, so she sat down at her little desk and wrote a letter: 'My Dears!... Oistrakh's such a charming little boy (his mother's Bulgarian). He's extremely engaging, not just with his playing, but with his behaviour too, and his appearance. When you watch him play, you just want to kiss him like you do Alinka. We've noticed that all the violinists from the USSR have something in their mouths while they're playing. Probably some kind of tranquilizer. Even so, he was nervous playing the Bach. He got a very warm reception from the audience. He played some things brilliantly, but not everything. His *Oberek* was good, but without any oomph. Nevertheless, nearly all the jurors gave him the highest mark.'[2]

The first prize did in fact go to Igor Oistrakh, with whom Grażyna soon met up again during the Long-Thibaud International Competition in Paris.

One of the pieces that the musicians were able to choose to play in the second round of the Henryk Wieniawski Violin Competition was Grażyna Bacewicz's *Polish Caprice* for solo violin.

'Give up the violin and be done with it!'

In 1953 Grażyna Bacewicz decided to give up her career as a concert violinist. She did later make an exception, just for premieres of her own compositions, including her *Humoresque* for violin and piano, her *Partita* for violin and piano, and her *Sonata No. 2* for solo violin. She took a long time to come to this decision, and she reveals her thought processes in her short story, 'Jesteśmy na remi' ('We're calling it quits').

'It might seem a straightforward matter. You want to give up violin? Give it up and be done with it! What's there to say? But that's not how it goes. A long-standing communion with one's instrument is suggestive of a marriage. Is it easy to leave your husband or wife after your silver wedding anniversary? Not easy! Even if you'd really like to. So I was putting off making a final decision. And then this cat turned up at home, a little kitten. He was so lovely and funny. Everyone at home really liked him. He, however, could not stand the violin. Whenever I picked it up, he'd start growling like a dog, and as soon as I made a sound on it, he'd race under the cupboard shrieking.

'I obviously couldn't have the kitten sitting under the cupboard all the time.

'So the matter became resolved of its own accord.'[4]

Symphony No. 4 and a ballet

In 1953 Grażyna Bacewicz composed a few important pieces, including *Symphony No. 4*, *Piano Sonata No. 2*, and music for the ballet *Z chłopa król* (*The Peasant King*). Though her home was still filled with sadness, daily life carried on as normal. Grażyna would take advantage of any available free time away from her public activities, shut herself up in her room, draw the curtains and, enveloped in semi-darkness, start to compose.

Then on 5 March 1953 all the loudspeakers that hung in the streets announced the death of Joseph Stalin. The streets began teeming with processions that had been organized by workplaces. Stalinism, a cruel and repressive totalitarian system, gradually began to thaw. On 9 March Maria wrote: 'Really lovely, the weather. Due to Stalin's funeral, meetings, parades, rallies, town packed, crowds, mourning etc.'[1]

A month later, Grażyna received some good news: 'The Polish Composers' Union [ZKP] has sent its assessment of the ballet, *The Peasant King*, which the Commissioned Compositions Committee at the Ministry of Culture and Art had commissioned. It was approved by the Executive Board of the ZKP at a meeting on 8 April 1953, and the fee has yet to be agreed,' Maria recorded meticulously.[1]

Now that she was a bit calmer, following the outcome for her ballet music, Grażyna was able to return to working on her *Symphony No. 4*, finishing both pieces simultaneously. She worked very intensively throughout the following month. She delivered the finished music to her publisher, PWM, who then sent her proofs for correction. She finally completed checking the proofs of both large scores on 17 May 1953.

Symphony No. 4 consists of four movements (*Appassionato*, *Adagio*, *Scherzo vivace*, *Adagio mesto*) and is written for a large symphony orchestra. Despite its neoromantic sound, the germs of sonorism* can be heard, showing the direction in which Bacewicz would be taking her compositions.

Grażyna Bacewicz dedicated her *Symphony No. 4* to Grzegorz Fitelberg, but he did not live to conduct it. Its premiere took place on 15 January 1954 in Kraków, with Bohdan Wodiczko conducting the Kraków Philharmonic

---

* Series Editor's note: Sonorism was a compositional technique, particularly applied to Polish music of the 1950s and 1960s, and effectively defined by the theorist Józéf M. Chomiński as putting 'sonorous values' in the foreground, so that timbre and texture take precedence over pitch, through devices such as tone clusters and glissandi.

Orchestra. Three months later, with Witold Krzemieński conducting, the piece was performed in Warsaw, along with Andrzej Panufnik's *Heroic Overture* and Kazimierz Serocki's *Trombone Concerto*.

'The evening…a whole bunch of us – spent at the Roma at the 23rd symphonic concert. A beautiful symphony – a great work and a great achievement for Grażyna. We were absolutely delighted with Grażyna's success and all the congratulations. For us, every evening of that kind is a hugely joyful experience,' Maria noted.[1]

7 Achievements and Losses

Beautiful Paris and painful news

In June 1953 Grażyna set off for Paris to serve as a juror at the Long-Thibaud International Competition. While she was there, she gave concert performances with Sergiusz Nadgryzowski and Henryk Sztompa. She wrote home: 'I effectively finish work on the fifteenth. Then, on the twenty-fourth I'm playing at the Embassy, and in between times, all I have is parties, oh, and the piano competition. On the fifteenth, De Vito's playing! I'll try to go and see her.

'It's funny the way it's turned out, that at the competition I've been Oistrakh's translator (because he doesn't always have his translator with him). Anyway, we feel like old friends (from that competition back in Warsaw). We're just awaiting the results from the first round. I don't know if I wrote and told you that the chair of the jury is Calvet – first violin in the famous Calvet Quartet, which he had to disband after he had an accident with his hand. They warned me not to mention the quartet, as he finds it distressing.

'We heard today that Ficio's died. What happened? We don't have any details yet. How are you all? Is everything all right? It seems that Sztompka and I still have another performance on the 25th at the Maison de la Pensée.

'I've been stuffing myself with oranges (every time I eat one, I think of Alinka and Grandma), and strawberries as well. As regards food, we're really well catered for.

Shkolnikova* from the USSR played brilliantly. The French are terribly proud that the Russians have travelled to this competition of theirs. And they have, in fact, floored the French.

---

*   Nelli Shkolnikova (1928–2010), a Soviet violinist and teacher, left to settle in Australia in 1982.

'Paris is as beautiful as ever. I gave some of my sheet music to Szeryng, who is now a Mexican citizen. I don't understand what happened to Fić. Had he been ill, or did he die suddenly?'[2]

The death of Grzegorz Fitelberg on 10 June 1953 had shocked everyone. Maria had reported in her journal: 'He died today, during the night – Fitelberg passed away most peacefully. He attended a meeting yesterday in Warsaw and spoke with and telephoned various friends and acquaintances. The funeral is on the thirteenth, on Saturday at Powązki Cemetery. Farewell speeches have already been given by Lutosławski, Sokorski, Gadomski, with two orchestras playing: the Katowice and Warsaw ones – Bach, Beethoven, and Chopin. Earlier they bid him farewell with pomp and ceremony in Katowice, in his last place of great, intensive work as Polish Radio's highly distinguished, long-serving conductor.'[1]

On 30 June 1953, after nearly a month-long stay in Paris, Grażyna Bacewicz returned home. She stayed up till two in the morning, relaying her impressions to her family. She had got to know Arthur Rubinstein, who had been delighted with her playing and her compositions. He even asked her for her photograph and assorted pieces. His whole family – wife and children – turned out to be exceptionally agreeable.

After all their hard, intensive work, they were all (including Kiejstut and Halszka) able to take a break along with the rest of the family during the holidays. Just as they did every year, the family went to Koszelówka and stayed by the lake. They swam, sunbathed, went blackberry and mushroom-picking, rode their bikes, played volleyball, and when it rained, they played hearts; but above all, they wrote countless postcards to their friends. Every so often, Grażyna would return to Warsaw to see to professional matters.

On their return, the family found a stack of congratulatory telegrams awaiting them, as Grażyna had been awarded the Knight's Cross of the Order of Polonia Restituta.

Towards the end of the year, three weeks after Gałczyński's death in Warsaw, Julian Tuwim died in Zakopane,* where Grażyna's whole family (minus Andrzej) was spending the Christmas holiday. During the farewell ceremony one of those in the guard of honour was Kiejstut Bacewicz. That evening, Grażyna wrote to her husband: 'We had Tuwim's funeral today. He

---

*   Translator's note: Konstanty Ildefons Gałczyzński (1905–1953) was a Polish poet whose most well-known works are his absurd humorous sketches for the Green Goose Theatre.

Julian Tuwim (1894–1953) was a major figure in Polish literature. He co-founded the Skamander group of experimental poets and set up the cabaret Picador. He was a prolific poet, a writer of satirical cabaret sketches, and a translator of Russian poetry. His children's poetry has been translated into many languages and continues to be extremely popular in Poland.

died suddenly after the *halniak** (aortic rupture). I wonder if the lady with the scythe will stop her rampage after the new year; or not. Alinka has been skiing with Wan. We've been doing a lot of walking – probably too much, as I can feel my heart. In fact, we're all in better shape.'[2]

Polish Overture

In the first half of 1954, Grażyna wrote her *Polish Overture*, her *Polish Caprice* (in a version for clarinet and piano), and her *Violin Concerto No. 5*. From Maria's notes, we know that she finished writing the *Overture* on 2 April 1954, then corrected the proofs of her *Symphony No. 3* for PWM; on 6 April she worked on the accompaniment of the *Caprice*, and straight after that she set to work on the changes to the ballet score of *The Peasant King* that Stanisław Miszczyk, ballet master at the Poznań Opera, was wanting to have.

A few days later, preparations were under way for Maria's birthday celebrations. It was a Saturday, and chilly outside, but it was cosy inside the apartment on Koszykowa Street, with delicious smells wafting out of the kitchen from the dishes that Maria was preparing.

'In the evening the Lutosławskis arrived with tulips, the Serockis with tulips, Baird with roses and Krenz with lilac. We had cold and warm dishes, supper with liqueurs, coffee, tea, cake, sweets. I didn't stay for supper, so they wouldn't feel uncomfortable fooling around; and they did joke about. They had a very merry time until two in the morning. Grażyna gave Krenz her new *Polish Overture*, that he's been wanting to get out there for ages,' wrote Maria.[1]

The *Overture*, dedicated to Kazimierz Sikorski, eventually had its premiere on 10 December 1954 in Kraków, with Bohdan Wodiczko conducting the Kraków Philharmonic Orchestra.

Violin Concerto No. 5 and ballet premiere

On 13 May 1954 in Poznań, Grażyna began attending rehearsals for the *Peasant King* ballet, on the invitation of ballet master Stanisław Miszczyk. As soon as she got home, she would start work on her *Violin Concerto No. 5*. The many notes on the subject in Maria's diary begin on 18 May 1954. The *Concerto* was eventually finished on 4 August 1954. Grażyna had been composing practically non-stop. She made an exception on 30 June, when she and her family drove out of the city to observe a solar eclipse, and a further exception for the ballet premiere on 25 July 1954.

In Poznań, Grażyna met up with her family, who had come up from their holiday in Koszelówka, especially to attend the event.

---

*   Translator's note: The 'halniak' (or 'halny') is a powerful and dangerous wind in the Tatra Mountains. The drastic change of atmospheric pressure that it brings with it is said to exacerbate the symptoms of all kinds of medical conditions, such as migraine, depression, heart dysfunction, and breathing problems.

'We set off for the Opera at 17.30 to watch the dress rehearsal of Grażyna's ballet *The Peasant King*,' Maria recorded in her diary. 'There was much excitement and great enthusiasm in the auditorium for Grażyna's ballet. The rehearsal went on till 10 p.m.; we came out dazzled; Grażyna pleased. She, Andrzej, and the Rudnickis were invited to dinner with Bierdiajew, where they discussed amendments to *The King* in scene three. The next day, in the evening, *The Peasant King* exceeded our long-awaited expectations. Our excellent conductor Bierdiajew and the master of choreography, Miszczyk, staged a splendid performance: beautiful, rich décor and costumes; first-rate dancers. The libretto by Artur Maria Swinarski went down well. The beautiful auditorium at the Opera was packed to the rafters. And then the flowers started raining down, and congratulations and telegrams, etc. In a word: a great success. And such a wonderful evening for us, an unforgettable experience. At such joyful and happy times like this, I always feel so sorry that our Vit isn't with us, and I used to feel that about Daddy too, that they haven't been able to experience it all with us.'[1]

On their return from Poznań, the whole family, this time including Grażyna, returned to the countryside; yet instead of doing sweet nothing on holiday, the composer brought her work with her and wrote out for herself the solo parts of her *Violin Concerto No.5*, which the board of the Polish Composers' Union had approved for public performance back in August.

Bang into a tree

On Sunday, 26 September 1954, the whole family was involved in a serious car accident. We know exactly what happened from Maria's journal:

'It was pouring in the morning, but by 9 a.m. we were in Andrzej's car on our way to Koszelówka. Grażyna didn't want to go and advised against it. We got there safely at midday. The whole family was there. We gave them some knick-knacks and sweets. They rustled up a quick dinner and gave us some purple plums, apples, nuts, sunflowers, butter, and bread. We said the warmest of goodbyes and, at 2 p.m., we set off for Warsaw in good weather. Grażyna told Alinka to sit in the middle, not on the outside. After 3 p.m., half a kilometre outside Sochaczew, on a wide, empty road, a lorry with a driver who was probably drunk pulled out from behind our car and pulled in so quickly and so close to our car that Andrzej suddenly had to swerve to the right. The wheel hit a large stone in the road and the car was flung with full force into a tree, on the side where Grażyna had been sitting.

'Alinka and I blacked out completely, though in our heads we heard the terrible din of the crashing car and the shattered windscreens. When we came to, the scene was horrific: Grażyna lying in the wet road with her face and head caked in blood, unable to move; she was saying: "I've broken my pelvis." Alinka's face and right hand were covered in blood. Wanda had been hurled into the ditch, fortunately landing on her rear, so that she had only sustained bruising, but her right hand was deeply wounded. Andrzej was completely at a loss as to what to do with Grażyna who was losing more and more blood and could neither sit nor lie down, or with Wanda, who was on the point of passing out.

'It was Alinka who brought Wanda round by slapping her across the face. Not a living soul, nor a drop of water on the road. When I fell over in the car wreck, I knocked my arm, my side, and my hands. There was blood everywhere in the car: on our clothes, on the floor, all around, wherever you looked. The car smashed to smithereens. A dozen or so minutes passed by like that. Fortunately, there was a passing car with two architects in it; they immediately turned round and drove back to Sochaczew to call for an ambulance, which arrived quickly and drove Grażyna carefully, Andrzej too, to the hospital in Sochaczew. Then the architects, Mr Ponikowski and Mr Zatorski, took care of the rest of us. First of all, they drove us to the hospital in Warsaw, at number 59 Nowogrodzka Street, so we could get bandaged up, and then home. The care and the support they gave us was extraordinary. We heard from Andrzej that Grażyna wasn't to be moved till the morning. She's had lots of stitches, as she has eight gashes on her head (one of them 6 cm in length and going right down to the bone) and on her forehead, face and chin – four smaller gashes. She was brave during the operation, but after the morphine and various injections she felt unwell… Andrzej came out of this unfortunate catastrophe unscathed – his hand a bit swollen and a bruise on his ear.'[1]

Years later, looking back at it from a distance, Grażyna described the event in her short story '*Ona już bredzi*' ('She's Delirious Now'): 'I was in a bad way, especially for the first two weeks. There were even some "borderline" moments. And that's precisely when I was protected by a wave of sounds, playing obsessively in my head. The opening of Bach's *Fugue in F Minor*. Always that one. It constituted a thread, that I clung on to tightly, so as not to be dragged over to the other side. When I had previously been unwell, that same music had saved me. I wonder how it is going to be at my last moment. Will we remain faithful to each other – that music and I?'[4]

Grażyna Bacewicz spent several months in hospital. Then she had a long period of recovery at home. Meanwhile, the outside world had been changing somewhat. People were feeling the 'thaw', the slogans of socialist realism eroding. Just before Christmas 1954, Grażyna wrote a letter to her friend Maria Dziewulska: 'During my illness I have learned to distinguish between those things that are important and those that are less so. Amongst the ones I consider less important are any personal ambitions or group ones. I would even include a poorer concert performance among the less important things in life. Among the more important things, I would include a stubborn, five-year resistance (because that's how long it's been) to the directives to not play so-called formalist music.'[8]

Second Festival of Polish Music

In 1955 the second Festival of Polish Music took place: a very large affair. This time the event spanned a longer period, running from 17 January to 20 May, and taking in 163 symphony concerts, in which 119 composers took part. The organisers were Tadeusz Baird, Kazimierz Serocki, Andrzej Dobrowolski, and Włodzimierz Kotoński. A fair number of Grażyna's compositions were performed during the festival: *Symphony No. 4*, *Concerto for String Orchestra*, *Violin Concertos Nos 2, 4,* and *5*, *Piano Concerto*, *Piano Quintet No. 1*, *Sonata No. 4 for Violin and Piano*, and the *Suite* from her ballet *The Peasant King*. The first day of the festival saw hurricane-force snowstorms raging throughout the whole of Europe, but the premiere of Grażyna's latest concerto took place all the same: 'We all went to the Roma Theatre for a symphony concert, where Wanda Wiłkomirska played Grażyna's *Violin Concerto No. 5* and Rowicki conducted. A difficult concerto, but a wonderful one, and Wanda played with great care. It was a great success. Grażyna was given flowers and congratulations. We came back in excellent spirits and chatted about the concert until late into the night,' wrote Maria.[1]

On a frosty Monday morning, on 21 February 1955, Grażyna and Andrzej set off for the ceremonial opening of the rebuilt Warsaw Philharmonic (henceforth known as the National Philharmonic). At that time Grażyna was finishing work on her *Sonatina* for piano. On 24 February 1955 she eventually sent it, along with a letter, to Arthur Rubinstein at his New York address.

Sad news arrived in March: the death of Professor Józef Jarzębski, her former violin teacher and one of the three musicians whom she had portrayed in her *Caricatures for Orchestra*. Maria noted the following: '8 March 1955: Grażyna is composing. Then, with Wanda and Andrzej to the service at the cathedral for Józef Jarzębski and his committal in Powązki Cemetery next to Barcewicz's grave – his former friend. The funeral was a most ceremonious occasion with lots of priests, and his brother, a priest, leading the proceedings, lots of flowers, eulogies, delegations from assorted music schools, his family, friends, acquaintances, and others.'[1]

Of Grażyna's three close mentors, there was now only Kazimierz Sikorski left.

In the middle of March 1955, musical Warsaw was living and breathing nothing but the V International Chopin Piano Competition. Grażyna and Andrzej went to hear the third round. As guest of honour at the competition, Elisabeth of Bavaria, Queen of Belgium, made an appearance at the Philharmonic. Maria commented in her journal: 'They're making a right spectacle of her here, whereas in Belgium and Paris people don't even notice her. It's so ludicrous.'[1] At every opportunity, Grażyna's mother liked to stress her positivistic worldview, expressing impatience with people who did not work hard every day to leave behind something of value to humanity.

The Queen's presence did, however, affect Grażyna's plans. She had been spending every available minute composing and transcribing her *Sonatina* for piano and her *Sonatina* for oboe and piano; and then, on 17 March 1955, she received a phone call from the Ministry of Culture and Art. A secretary announced: 'The Queen invites Madame Grażyna Bacewicz and a few other artists to a reception at the Belgian Embassy on Saturday 19 March at 19.00 hours.'

Andrzej drove Grażyna, Wanda Wiłkomirska, and Tadeusz Wroński to the royal reception. Grażyna could not bear long ceremonies of this kind, so she and Wiłkomirska left early, and Minister Sokorski arranged for the ladies to be driven home.

Despite this and various other interruptions, Grażyna eventually finished her *Sonatina* for piano, and got to hear it performed on 9 May 1955, at a concert of chamber music where she was one of the performers. Maria noted that: 'Though Grażyna has been ill recently, she looked very lovely. She played her *Sonata No. 4* with Tutik.* It was very well received and there were lots of flowers. Szymonowicz played Grażyna's *Sonatina* on the piano, and the Kraków Quartet did a brilliant performance of Grażyna's *Quartet No. 4*, which was awarded first prize in Liège. Grażyna sent each of them a bunch of flowers. After the concert, a professor from Graz, Hans Wamlek, who loves Grażyna's compositions, and the Rudnickis partied at ours. They ate, drank, and had a very merry time joking around.'[1]

That same year, Grażyna Bacewicz received the Minister for Culture and Art's Prize for her *Symphony No. 4*, *Violin Concerto No. 3*, and *String Quartet No. 3*. She was also awarded the Order of Polonia Restituta Commander's Cross and the Tenth Anniversary Medal of the Polish People's Republic.

Songs

'On 18 May 1955, Grażyna finished transcribing two of her songs: *The Little Magpie* and *My Head Hurts*, and gave these to the singer, Maria Drewniakówna, for her to prepare for a concert,' wrote Maria.[1] Both songs were jokey in nature, and in terms of sound too. Amusing onomatopoeic effects appear in the ostensibly simple *Magpie*, where the melody and harmony move between the modal line of the voice, tonality and polytonality.

Early in the morning of 25 May 1955, Maria Drewniakówna arrived at Grażyna's flat on Koszykowa Street, seeking advice from Grażyna on how to interpret the songs. Maria, who was sitting in the kitchen, heard Drewniakówna sing the following pieces one after another: *Mamidło* (*Illusion*), *Inna* (*Different*), *Smuga cienia* (*Shadow Line*), *Boli mnie głowa* (*My Head Hurts*), and *Mała sroczka* (*The Little Magpie*). The concert took place

---

*   Translator's note: 'Tutik' is a diminutive of 'Kiejstut', Grażyna's brother.

on 31 May 1955. Grażyna described the event in her short story 'Scandal', while her mother also wrote her own account: 'In the afternoon we went to the Journalists' Hall at number 3 Foksal Street, to a musical evening, "Meet the Composer". There were lots of people we knew there: the Rudnickis, the Łosakiewiczes, the Rostafińskis, the Szczepańskis, and many other musicians. In the first half there was a speech by the president of the ZKP, Sikorski, and then they were supposed to play tapes of Grażyna's *Concerto for Strings* (third movement), the *Scherzo* from *Symphony No. 3*, and *String Quartet No. 4*; but due to some oversight, they put on God only knows what. They had mixed up the pieces, so some kind of shouting and banging came out. It was absolute hell. So, the directors are obviously going to get into deep trouble over what they did. In the second part Maria Drewniakówna sang (and Tutik accompanied) five of Grażyna's songs. She did it very well. Then Grażyna and Tutik played her *Sonata No. 4 for Violin and Piano*, *Mazovian Dance*, *Lullaby*, and *Oberek*. They played brilliantly, and there was non-stop applause from the full concert hall. The atmosphere was very warm and lovely. Then there was a cheery discussion, with clever questions, naïve ones too, and a request from the audience for Grażyna to play the piano. So, she played one of the movements from her *Sonatina*. Lots more noisy applause.'[1]

Not surprisingly, as was usually the case after a concert, the whole group drove over to the flat on Koszykowa Street. They had great fun, partying until one in the morning.

Lady Vice-President of the Polish Composers' Union

At the start of June 1955, at the Eighth Annual General Meeting of the Union of Polish Composers (ZKP), Tadeusz Baird and Kazimierz Serocki (Vice-Presidents at the time) proposed a motion for the upcoming meeting of the Executive Board of the ZKP about organizing a permanent festival to be known as Warszawska Jesień Muzyczna (Warsaw's Musical Autumn). The plan was to put Polish audiences in touch with western music, and following years of Stalinism, to wrench it out of its isolation and, more importantly, defeat the ideology of socialist realism. Elections took place, and Kazimierz Sikorski was elected President once again. Baird and Serocki did not stand, as a year earlier, they had endorsed Andrzej Panufnik's candidacy, but Panufnik had unexpectedly emigrated to the West. Those appointed to the posts of Vice-President were Grażyna Bacewicz, Father Hieronim Feicht, Witold Rudziński, and Andrzej Dobrowolski.

Not long after the congress ended, the project of organizing a new festival was approved by the highest authorities, and the machinery of frequent meetings at the Polish Composers' Union and deliberations at the Ministry of Culture and Art was set into motion.

That day, 6 June 1955, Grażyna came home tired. As she sipped her tea, she related the proceedings to her mother.

'You know, mum, in the elections I got the highest number of votes for president. But I wouldn't accept; I asked Sikorski to be president again.'

'What do you mean – you turned the post down?' Maria asked.

'I've been made one of the vice-presidents.'

'Wiechowicz has sent you a huge bouquet of flowers, and a card's arrived from Genia Umińska from Leipzig, saying that she played your *Concerto No. 3* with Hermann Abendroth. He conducted brilliantly. It was a huge success and they recorded it on tape.'

Maria placed a postcard on the table. She liked looking at the various postcards that came in from all over the world.

On 14 June 1955 she found a new postcard in the mail and told her daughter: 'Grażynko; we've had news from Wanda Wiłkomirska. She writes that in Turkey she played your pieces with the pianist Jadwiga Szamotulska, and she sends her warmest greetings.'

A smiling Grażyna replied, 'I'll send her a thank you card when we're on holiday.'

The whole family and their friends had great fun in Zakopane. They went on excursions up into the mountains, and they entertained themselves indoors when the weather was rainy. The composer kept busy too. She asked her husband to send her some manuscript paper and she found herself 'a room by the hour with piano', as the competition for a vocal piece set to words by Mickiewicz was fast approaching, in commemoration of the hundredth anniversary of the poet's death. Only in mid-August did she let herself be persuaded to go on an outing to Hala Gąsienicowa with Wanda, Alinka, and Kiejstut, under careful supervision from Wawrzyniec Żuławski.

As they were walking along Krupówki Street in Zakopane, the 'ladies' took the opportunity to get weighed. The petite Maria weighed barely 35 kilos; Wanda 57.5 kilos and Grażyna (the tallest of them, with a height of 1m 63cm) 52.5 kilos. The sporty Zakopane lifestyle helped the ladies keep their slim figures.

Bells in Warsaw; *Partita* in Kraków

On her return to Warsaw on 1 September 1955, Grażyna got down to composing her *String Quartet No. 5*. Soon afterwards she went back to work on her songs to Mickiewicz's texts: *Dzwon i dzwonki* (*Bell and Chimes*) and *Nad wodą wielką I czystą* (*By the Great and Clear Water*). For the first of these songs, she received a commendation in the 'Mickiewicz' competition. (The first prize was awarded to Stefan Kisielewski; second prize to Piotr Perkowski.)

In October 1955, Grażyna started work on a new composition: 'Grażyna is composing a *Partita* for violin and piano: *Prelude, Toccata, Intermezzo,*

Rondo' wrote Maria. 'She is going to be playing it with Tutik in November at PWM's tenth-anniversary celebrations in Kraków'[1]. Grażyna went at her work on the *Partita* with exceptional energy. On 22 October, she transcribed the piano part for Kiejstut, so that he could take it to Łódź to practise.

A few days later, on 2 November, Kiejstut let Grażyna know that he had already learned the accompaniment both to *Bells* and to the *Partita*. Soon after his letter, he arrived in person, to rehearse his sister's new composition in her presence. A few days later he arrived with the singer for the premiere of *Bell and Chimes*. The event took place on 7 November 1955 in Warsaw: 'Tutik arrived around midday with the soprano Mrs Lidia Skowron. They sang after breakfast – Grażyna's instructions to *Bell and Chimes*; then dinner, rehearsal, afternoon tea, and at 7 p.m. we all went to the Chopin Institute for the chamber concert. Skowron sang very nicely. She went down very well. She was given flowers.'[1]

On 15 December 1955 Grażyna picked up her pen and wrote a dedication on the first page of her music: 'To dear Mrs Lidia Skowron, first excellent performer of *Bells*, Grażyna Bacewicz'.

The publisher PWM's tenth-anniversary celebrations took place on 19 and 20 November 1955. On the previous day the board of the Polish Composers' Union had met for a plenary meeting in Kraków. The programme committee of PWM had planned two concerts with numerous first performances. According to Maria's notes, on the first day, pieces by Stanisław Skrowaczewski, Jan Krenz, Tadeusz Baird, Stefan Kisielewski, Witold Rudziński, and Grażyna Bacewicz were played (her *Partita* for violin and piano), and, on the second day, works by Andrzej Cwojdziński, Maria Dziewulska, Stefania Lachowska, and Tomasz Sikorski.

String Quartet No. 5

The concert in Kraków was very successful, and as soon as Grażyna returned to Warsaw on 21 November (as ever, without taking any rest) she returned to work on her *String Quartet No. 5*, which she had begun after the holidays. Her work was constantly being interrupted by various commitments, be they meetings at the Polish Composers' Union, or sundry other appointments. At one of the meetings, she found out that a group of musicians and writers was planning a trip to India. The outline of this long-distance trip was slowly taking shape. Grażyna had been taking English lessons for some time. The prospect of the trip, along with the fast-approaching Christmas holiday, gave her even more motivation. 'The twelfth of December… Grażyna is rooted to the spot composing her *Quartet No. 5*. Wan,* after Radio, is spending hours queuing for oranges (there's been a new delivery for Christmas shoppers).'[1]

---

*   Translator's note: 'Wan' is a diminutive of 'Wanda', Grażyna's sister.

Just before Christmas 1955, on 20 December, Grażyna Bacewicz completed her *String Quartet No. 5*. She finished copying out the score in Zakopane. She arrived there on 23 December with Maria and Wanda, and met up with Kiejstut, Halszka, and assorted friends, including Professor Sikorski. After unpacking, they went into town to buy a small, token Christmas tree. Andrzej joined them the following day, and the whole family spent Christmas Eve together.

When, on 27 December, Professor Sikorski was about to return to Warsaw, his most talented pupil arrived at the railway station and handed him the score of her *String Quartet No. 5*, with the request that he take it to the Polish Composers' Union, where Marysia Łosakiewicz would pick it up and transcribe the different instrumental parts.

Before her big trip to India, Grażyna went over to Polish Radio to make a recording in the series *My Favourite Compositions*. These are the pieces she mentioned in the programme:

1. Bach: *Toccata and Fugue in D Minor* for organ
2. Brahms: first movement of his *Violin Sonata in G Major*
3. Ravel: *Pavane pour une enfante défunte*
4. Bartók: first movement of his *String Quartet No. 6*
5. Prokofiev: first movement of his *Piano Sonata No. 7*
6. Brahms: *Symphony No. 1 in C Minor*

8 Distant Travels and Family Matters

Trip to India

On 16 February 1956, Grażyna met up in Prague with several artists: composers, writers, and painters. From there the group set off for India, travelling via Zurich, Milan, and Rome, and on the return via Egypt. Years later, Grażyna shared her impressions of those days in a few of her short stories; Maria, on the other hand, wrote regular reports of the trip. Thanks to her, we know that before she set off, Grażyna had to have a series of compulsory injections against cholera, typhus, chickenpox, and malaria. She issued instructions to the family on domestic and budgetary matters. She also wrote a letter to Nadia Boulanger, thanking her warmly for fond memories of their earlier encounters and saying she was looking forward to her arrival in the autumn for the first International Festival of Contemporary Music.

Maria kept an eager eye out for postcards from her daughter, curious to read about her impressions of the 'fabulous trip'. On 23 February, she eventually received a postcard sent from Prague, followed by four more: two from Rome and two from New Delhi.

'You know, Wandziu,' she said to her younger daughter, 'they have sweltering heat in Delhi; there are never any storms. Grażyna is delighted with the way the women look, with their elegant refinement. She writes that they carry loads on their heads. She's not had much sleep, and if she just ate local cuisine, she would come back like a shadow. She sends her love to everyone.'

On 27 February 1956 the Polish delegation travelled by train to Agra, and on 2 March arrived in Calcutta (now called Kolkata). The trains were saloon-cars, and the sleeping conditions were comfortable.

DISTANT TRAVELS AND FAMILY MATTERS

The next lot of postcards reached Warsaw on 6 March 1956. Grażyna wrote that Prime Minister Jawaharlal Nehru and 'Raja Krishna'* had attended a concert and welcomed the Polish delegation. In her spare time, she basked in the sun, which she absolutely loved.

'She's so full of impressions that she doesn't know what to write about!' said Maria with excitement. 'She writes about the abundant wildlife, the trees shimmering with birds, squirrels, and monkeys, and the streets with camels and buffalo walking among the cars. Elegant buildings and miserable shacks exist side by side. The Polish delegation is staying in a lovely building, where the receptions take place. Everything seems dreamlike. She finds it interesting listening to Indian music, which she wasn't familiar with before. During the day the heat is sweltering, but it turns cold at night-time; fortunately, they have heaters.'

Grażyna's next letter came from Madras (known as Chennai since 1996). The city made a good impression on her; it was clean and well-maintained, but more importantly, it lay by the ocean. There was a heatwave, so the delegation of Polish artists was eager to sunbathe, although some confusion in the ranks might have been caused by news of the Polish President Bolesław Bierut's death. Neither Grażyna, nor her companions in far-away India were able to witness the crowds of people flocking to the front of the PZPR (Polish United Workers' Party) building where, over 48 hours, hundreds of thousands of citizens from different places of work had been coming to lay flowers and wreaths by the open coffin in which their deceased leader's body had been laid out for public viewing.

The last stage of the trip was Egypt. On 24 March 1956, Grażyna sent a telegram from Cairo with nameday wishes for Maria, and a week later she alighted from the train at the railway station in Warsaw, where she was greeted by her husband Andrzej, with a huge bouquet of flowers. Maria wrote: 'What joy on seeing each other! Despite her tiredness, Grażyna was looking lovely; her face pink and filled-out. One could see how happy she was. Straight away over breakfast, she started telling us all about her interesting, wonderful, unforgettable trip. She brought us some souvenirs back from Delhi, Agra, Bombay, Madras, Calcutta, Cairo, Rome, Venice, and Vienna. Sikorski came round in the evening, and over supper listened to Grażyna's hugely-interesting stories.'[1]

Grażyna's reminiscence of the trip was expressed in the music she wrote for Balwant Gargi's play, *The Indian Woman*,** which was recorded on 8 June 1956 in Poznań.

---

*   Translator's note: Grażyna Bacewicz is probably referring to Nehru's sister, Krishna, who married Gunottam (Raja) Hutheesing.
** Translator's note: Balwant Gargi's play, *Kesro*, was titled *The Indian Woman* in Poland.

Vist to Paris; another prize in Liège; global Warsaw

Soon after her daughter's return from India, Maria underwent an operation on her leg. It was the first time in her life that she found herself in hospital, as she had given birth to all her children at home. By an unfortunate coincidence, Andrzej Biernacki was also then in the hospital as a patient. Grażyna soon forgot about her travels to exotic countries.

In her journal, Maria wrote: 'Grażynka came running up to me, did everything for me, fed me, and then ran off to the other end of the hospital to Andrzej; and from there she went to the ZKP to do organizational work for the composition competition.'[1]

The competition was to take place between 16 and 19 April 1956. Grażyna was the Chair of the Organizational Committee and a member of the jury, along with Jean Absil, Pál Kadosa, Witold Lutosławski, Kazimierz Sikorski, and Michael Tippett.

Grażyna's sending of her *String Quartet No. 5* to the String Quartet Competition in Liège had turned out to be an important move. The piece won second prize and was performed by the Quatuor Municipal de Liège. She travelled to the awards ceremony with her daughter Alina and visited Paris *en route*. There she attended to matters relating to the organization of the festival concerts that would soon be taking place in Warsaw. On her return, in a radio interview on 2 October 1956, Grażyna declared that there was great interest from all over the world in the Warsaw festival, and that she had spent three weeks in Paris on business matters, to discuss the Orchestre National de la Radiodiffusion Française's appearance in Warsaw. She visited lots of people, including her dear former professor, Nadia Boulanger.

The First International Festival of Contemporary Music (the name 'The Warsaw Autumn' was given at the next festival, two years later) ran from 10 to 20 October 1956. It took place in the atmosphere of thaw that followed Stalin's death and the subsequent changes in the Soviet Union. On 25 February 1956, at the Twentieth Congress of the Communist Party of the Soviet Union, details of Nikita Khrushchev's secret speech relating to Stalin's crimes had come to light.

The Polish President Bolesław Bierut's sudden death in Moscow in March 1956 was followed in June by riots that swept through Poznań. All these events led to a split within the Polish United Workers' Party and to Władysław Gomułka's team coming into power.

Attending the festival in Warsaw were the aforementioned French radio orchestra, the Vienna Symphony Orchestra, and ensembles from Bucharest, Brno, and Moscow. There were also performances by the National Philharmonic Symphony Orchestra and the Silesian Philharmonic Orchestra from Katowice (still known at the time as Stalinogród). One of the guest performers in Warsaw was David Oistrakh.

Three of Grażyna's compositions were performed at the festival: *The Polish Overture* (played by the USSR State Symphony Orchestra and conducted by Nikolai Anosov), her *String Quartet No. 4* (played by the Quatuor Parrenin), and her *Concerto for String Orchestra* (with Jean Martinon conducting the French radio orchestra).

Ten Concert Études for piano

On 18 October 1956, just before the festival concerts, Grażyna held official receptions for Nadia Boulanger, Zygmunt Mycielski, and the Lutosławskis. Meanwhile, Poland's politics were in turmoil. Following Gomułka's first speech in which he had condemned Stalinism and announced that there were to be reforms and democratization of the political system, the Poles had been counting on a loosening-up of terror tactics from the authorities, but their hopes were soon dashed, and by December, further riots were breaking out.

After the festival, Grażyna got down to composing – piano studies this time – even though there was a lot going on at home. On 10 November 1956 Wanda got married, and the reception took place in Koszykowa Street.

After this, her composing was interrupted by preparations for Christmas, which the family, as always, planned to spend in the Tatra Mountains. Before leaving, they had had to get Christmas packages ready to send to Koszelówka, as well as the monthly parcel to Andrzej's now-ailing aunt in Marynin, Zofia Widulińska, at whose home the family had taken refuge during the war. So the women had to stand in endless shop queues to buy food and sweets.

After returning from a fairytale Zakopane, Grażyna finished her piano composition. The cycle of *Ten Concert Études* consists of pieces that differ from each other in terms of technique and expression. Each one was written with a view to practising a specific problem of execution (playing knotty passages, or two-note chords, tri-chords, or quartal chords) yet in their entirety they form a cyclical whole. *Études No. 5* and *No. 8* move along at a slow pace; the climactic moments appear in *Études No. 6* and *No. 10*. The whole cycle premiered at the Second Warsaw Autumn in 1958, where it was performed by Regina Smendzianka.

The *Ten Concert Études*, along with Grażyna's other études, her *Children's Suite*, her sonatas, and her later *Little Triptych*, together form a large body of solo pieces for piano. In all, the composer wrote around thirty pieces for piano.

Symphonic Variations

The beginning of 1957 brought the Bacewicz family the sad news of the death of their long-time friend, Edmund Rudnicki, on 17 January. The funeral service took place on 22 January in Warsaw, and then in Kraków in the Pauline Church on the Rock. The funeral itself was a grand affair, and he was laid to rest in Rakowicki Cemetery near his parents' grave.

In the spring, on 12 April, Grażyna got down to transcribing her recently finished *Symphonic Variations*. This composition seems to be a bridge between her neoclassical style and the sonoristic style of her symphonic works. It comprises a theme and eight variations. The theme is made up of a collection of motifs, of which three come to the fore and hold the entire fabric of the piece together.

The composer was still working on the piece on 28 April, when at midnight she set off for Katowice for the recording of her *Symphony No. 3*, conducted by Jan Krenz. The same conductor would conduct the premiere of her *Symphonic Variations* at the next Warsaw Autumn on 30 September 1958.

From 19 May 1957, Grażyna Bacewicz was in Kraków, to take part in the Council of Contemporary Music, and then on 21 May in a PWM concert, where Regina Smendzianka gave the premiere of seven of Grażyna's *Ten Concert Études*. She then went on to Katowice to sit on the jury for the Grzegorz Fitelberg Composition Competition.

In the shadow of the mountains: *Violin Concerto No. 6*

The Bacewicz 'ladies' spent July 1957 in Zakopane. On her return to Warsaw, Grażyna had a none too pleasant 'visit' from a member of the security services. On 6 August 1957, she complained bitterly to her husband: 'I am furious, because it's clear that my trip to Italy is once again creating suspicion. I've just had a "little visit". In a more refined form, perhaps. They do it well, because I didn't catch on to begin with, but I didn't say anything foolish at all. He pretended to be a doctor who had come from Lviv and was supposedly looking for you, so I even let him into the study. When I suddenly realized, I immediately broke off the conversation; and when I closed the door behind him. I couldn't help swearing out loud, which he must have heard. What a brute! That spoiled my mood for work, because it is unpleasant, after all. What's it all about? I don't understand! I'm not writing to them in Zakopane about this. Don't worry! I'm over it now.'[2]

On 18 August, news spread that Wawrzyniec Żuławski had lost his life in the Alps on Mont Blanc du Tacul. Together with seven other mountaineers, and connected by a rope to Stanisław Biel, he had set off on a rescue mission to find three fellow climbers who had gone missing: his friend Stanisław Groński and two Yugoslavians. When she heard the news, Grażyna returned to Zakopane as fast as she could.

'At midday, the family went to pick Grażyna up from the station,' wrote the composer's mother. 'She looked very pale and upset about the tragic death of Wawrzyniec Żuławski. A wonderful man, and a great friend of Grażyna's.'[1]

The following day, tribute articles and memories of Wawrzyniec Żuławski appeared in the press, variously describing him as Tatra-mountain-climber and Alpine mountaineer, president of the Mountaineering Club, conqueror of the most difficult routes in the Tatra Mountains, composer, writer, music critic, teacher, and Home Army insurgent during the Warsaw Uprising.

'On 21 August Grażyna sent Żuławski's mother a long telegram of condolences, and then in the afternoon she wrote out her *Violin Concerto No. 6* with orchestra, that she's currently composing,' recalled Maria.[1]

On 28 August 1957, Grażyna asked the Żuławski family to suspend the search for his body, which it was believed had come to rest below a dozen or so metres of snow and ice, not far from the place where his injured partner, Stanisław Biel, had been found. The family decided that flowers would be laid there, and that on more accessible terrain, either a monument would be erected, or a memorial plaque laid. On 1 September 1957, a wreath of flowers was dropped from an aeroplane flown by the pilot Firmin Guiron (president of the Aéro Club du Mont Blanc and famous for flying over glaciers), the highest tribute paid by Wawrzyniec Żuławski's fellow alpine mountaineers to their heroic friend.

On 7 September 1957 Grażyna and other musicians attended a memorial mass for the soul of their friend in the Church of the Holy Cross in Warsaw. Present there were Wawrzyniec Żuławski's mother, his family and other friends, representatives of the Polish Composers' Union, and the executive board members of the Mountaineering Club.

The following day, which Maria remembered well, 'Grażyna finished her *Violin Concerto No. 6* with orchestra. Desperately tired, she went to bed early.'[1]

Grażyna later withdrew this composition from her catalogue. It is not known why. From Maria's notes we learn that, on 9 September 1957, Grażyna 'asked the Polish Composers' Union about the possibility of transcribing the score and instrumental parts from her *Violin Concerto No. 6*. Gimpel is interested in it, but we can't send him the one handwritten copy.'[1] Just before she left for Italy on Warsaw Autumn business, Grażyna asked her family to send the score to Władysław Szpilman, who was in contact with Gimpel.

We do not know more about what happened at the time to Bacewicz's *Violin Concerto No 6*. It could be that the composer came to the conclusion that she would in fact prefer not to show the world the dramatic emotions it portrayed, which she was going through then. The composition had to wait several decades to have its first performance; the world premiere took place 62 years later in Warsaw on 6 December 2019. It was performed by Bartłomiej Nizioł and the National Philharmonic Orchestra, with Christoph König conducting.

Chair of the Jury of the Third Wieniawski Competition

As an exceptionally practical woman who thought about many of life's daily matters, Maria Modlińska made the following note: 'Grażyna is busy in town at the dressmaker's having clothes made and freshening up her wardrobe, essential for her three-week-long trip to Poznań for the Wieniawski Competition. As the Chair of the Competition and the Jury, she needs to be suitably attired. She is also working on her speeches.'[1]

The Third Wieniawski Competition in Poznań ran from the first to the fifteenth of December 1957. It had three rounds and was enriched by compositions from contemporary composers: Grażyna Bacewicz and Zbigniew Turski included. The members of the jury were Irena Dubiska, Eugenia Umińska, David Oistrakh, André Gertler, Louis Persinger, and honorary jury member Yehudi Menuhin.

On her return home, Grażyna found her mother seriously ill. The family had to change its plans and, this time, spend Christmas at home. On 18 December 1957 Maria wrote: 'I'm in bed. Grażyna and everyone are really looking after me. Andrzej and the doctors are giving me very tender medical care, and they're asking me to eat lots, but I can't. I've completely lost my appetite. Oistrakh has sent Grażyna a wonderful, huge bouquet of gorgeous white lilacs, and a little card.'[1]

Her mother's illness

In January 1958, Maria, now permanently bedridden, wrote in her journal: 'Grażyna is at the Philharmonic at a rehearsal of her *Piano Sonata*. The young pianist, Jasiński, is playing it very well.

'Everyone's out for the evening at the chamber concert. Grażyna's sonata went down very well, but then it is excellent. Grażyna came back with some beautiful carnations from the performer.'[1]

The daughters took it in turn to care for their mother, and Kiejstut and his wife Halszka frequently came up from Łódź. Amidst all her activities, Grażyna had less time for composing, but she did start writing a novel: 'A very original one, contemporary in form and spirit; full of wit and gentle irony; but probably only aimed at a narrow readership: musicians, i.e. those in the know about matters relating to the Polish Composers' Union, about composition, performance, and conducting, etc.', noted Maria. 'The humorous expressions with their own distinctive flavour, without any further clarification, would be unintelligible to the ordinary reader. Anyway, it's a very interesting novel.'[1]

Bacewicz's novel, later pieced together by her family, bears the title *O składaczach dźwięków i szmerów* (*Of Arrangers of Sounds and Murmurs*).

In the spring, on 10 March 1958, Andrzej Biernacki flew out to the United States of America, via Paris, as the first part of a four-month-long Rockefeller travel scholarship which he had been awarded. In New York he met up with Vytautas, which made Maria very happy, as she dreamed of seeing her son before she died. Unfortunately, her dream was never fulfilled, as Vytautas only obtained American citizenship, that would enable him to travel freely to Europe, a few years after his mother's death.

On 16 March 1958, Grażyna, who had been invited to be a juror in the First International Peter Tchaikovsky Violin Competition, departed for Moscow. In June, as the Polish delegate, she travelled to Strasbourg to attend the sessions and concerts of the World Music Days Festival of the International Society for Contemporary Music. Being far from home, she worried about the continuing decline in her mother's health. On 8 June, she sent a postcard to Stockholm, where her husband was at the time: 'Dear Andrzej, I arrived in Strasbourg tonight, with others (by train). I'm still worried about the situation at home. Mummy was in a bad way before I left. It all starts tomorrow. The sessions go on for five days (dammit); there are concerts every day, of course. How are things with you? Where will you be going after Sweden? Is everything all right? Lots of love Grażyna. When do you think you'll get back?'[2]

Maria tried to keep her journal going to the end of her life. Unfortunately, her notes became increasingly scanty and indecipherable. Her last entry on the first of July 1958 was to do with family matters. Less than three weeks later, Maria Modlińska died, on 18 July.

Grażyna described those painful days in a letter to Vytautas: 'We've not written and told you until now – it somehow escaped our minds to begin with, and then later we didn't really see the point – that Mummy is dying. When she was still able to speak, this is what she said to Kiej and Wan (I was lying nearby on the couch, as it was my turn to have a sleep; we'd brought these sleep shifts in for the last two and a half days; otherwise we'd never have coped; I was lying there, but I heard everything): that I have to be in charge of everything now, that I have more work than anyone else, so you're all to help me and listen to me. Later she added, jokingly, "Well, I've given my orders." Obviously, it would be silly of me to take these words the wrong way. I neither intend to order anyone around, nor impose anything on anyone. It's just that Mummy had well understood that essentially, even though I have a lot of work, I'm nanny to everyone in the family, whether they realize it or not. So I think she thought that I should be made head of the family.'[2]

Second Warsaw Autumn

'We're currently having our Festival of Contemporary Music,' wrote Grażyna to Vytautas in the autumn of 1958. 'Lots of visitors from abroad and performers. From the USA we've had the wonderful Juilliard Quartet. They played Bartók's fourth quartet, amongst other things. It's excellent music. There was lots of Schönberg, Berg, Webern, Bartók, and other new composers in the programme. There's going to be an evening of electronic music with Stockhausen, and today we have a wind quintet from Toulouse playing. But there's too much music. Fourteen concerts within nine days. Out of my pieces they've played the *Ten Concert Études*. That went well; but my *Symphonic Variations* – they didn't make much of an impact. My friend Lutosławski had great success with his *Funeral Music* in honour of Bartók. (Serial music.*) I'd like to get down to work now. But there's always something in the way.'[2]

After their mother's death, Grażyna's correspondence with her brother became even more intense, as if she were trying to make up for her mother's loss. In a letter from this period Grażyna shares her views on composing. 'Composing for me is like chiselling away at a rock, rather than transmitting to paper the sounds that I've imagined or been inspired by. Most composers work systematically, like bureaucrats. When we lack inspiration, we work with our technical skills; when we're inspired, we press on, little by little.'[2]

Elsewhere in the same letter, she describes the principles of twelve-tone technique: 'This kind of system gets rid of the ballast and teaches us to see voices as independent of each other, and to think polyphonically. Besides, mathematics is closer to abstraction than chaos is. I'm just saying, not trying to talk you into serialism. Anyway, I do know one thing – the way people used to compose, we're not allowed to do any more. However, we do need to be sincere. So, apart from some system within which we operate, we need to reject everything that readily imposes itself on us, and which isn't on some level innovative. This is how I move forward with my work, one bar at a time, after a twelve-hour day. What I'm basically doing is looking for "diamonds" in the sand. What will be the result? The devil only knows. Why are you so bothered about whether a piece reflects reality or not? One thing is certain: that when writing music, a composer can't think about that. Old Plato said that if a creator has anything else on his mind other than purely his own pleasure, then that's a bad thing!'[2]

In 1958, despite her mother's illness, Grażyna managed to compose her *Sonata No. 2* for solo violin and her *Music for Strings, Trumpets and Percussion*. She dedicated the latter to Jan Krenz.

---

*   Series Editor's Note. Although 'serialism' is a term initially used to denote repeating patterns in a composition, by the autumn of 1958, Bacewicz was referring specifically to the 12-tone technique pioneered by Schönberg, and employed by his 'Second Viennese School' colleagues Berg and Webern (all of whom appeared at this Festival of Contemporary Music). Instead of the previous concept of tonality, serial compositions employed a musical 'backbone' of the twelve tones of the chromatic scale arranged in a particular order, specific to each piece. Lutosławski's *Funeral Music* (in four sections) adopts a 12-tone row based exclusively on tritones and minor seconds. From this point on, Bacewicz herself occasionally used such serial techniques (notably in *String Quartet No. 6*).

'Maybe one day my "pieces" will be of use to someone'

In March 1959 in Kraków, Grażyna gave the premiere of her *Sonata No. 2* for solo violin. When she returned home to Warsaw, she worked on her radio opera: *Przygoda Krola Artura* (*The Adventure of King Arthur*). The libretto, based on an old Celtic legend, was written by Edward Fiszer. The premiere took place on 10 October 1959 with the Polish Radio Orchestra and the choir and soloists of the National Philharmonic, with Stefan Rachoń conducting. 'That whole period of recording the opera (three weeks) was a great pleasure for me, as everyone – Rachoń, the mixer, the soloists, and even the orchestra – was so enthusiastic about it, that they bent over backwards so it would all come out as well as possible. A funny kind of story (a very witty text),' wrote Grażyna in a letter to Maria Dziewulska [8]; while to Vytautas she explained: 'That opera that Kiej mentioned to you, it's for radio, but maybe in the future it'll be on television. It's 48 minutes long, but it could be made longer on stage with ballet.'[2]

On 14 September 1959, during the third Warsaw Autumn International Festival of Contemporary Music, the premiere of Bacewicz's *Music for Strings, Trumpets and Percussion* took place. It was performed by the Polish National Radio Symphony Orchestra with Jan Krenz conducting. Two days before the start of the festival, Grażyna shared the following thought with Vytautas: 'Throughout our lives, we are criticized by hundreds of people, and what does it matter? If we really took it to heart, we'd never write anything. My motto: try to do what I do as best I can, without thinking about the consequences, because we have no influence on them anyway. I can't, for instance, do anything about it if, in the future, people judge my work inferior to that of Brahms, for example. I am not as talented as he, and there's nothing that I can do about it. But despite that, maybe one day my "pieces" will be of use to someone for something, and that will do for me.'[2]

After the premiere of *Music for Strings, Trumpets and Percussion*, Grażyna Bacewicz had no need to worry about criticism from the public. On the contrary: the following year (1960) the piece was placed third at UNESCO's International Rostrum of Composers in Paris. The piece signals a new sound language in her compositions. Dynamic movement, dense sounds, and varied textures determine the form of the piece. The logic of the whole piece is self-evident. The lively opening *Allegro* is based on sonata form with a distinctive first theme. The second movement, *Adagio*, brings in a delicate game of textured sound patterns, with solo motifs played by different instruments; while the third movement, *Vivace*, is an explosion of different sounds.

The last decade of Grażyna Bacewicz's life was a time of creative synthesis. She composed many of her most important works during that period, including her *String Quartet No. 6*, *Pensieri notturni*, *Concerto for Large Symphony Orchestra*, *Cello Concerto No. 2*, *Quartet* for four cellos, the cantata *Akropolis*, *Violin Concerto No. 7*, *Piano Quintet No. 2*, *String Quartet No. 7*, *Musica sinfonica in tre movimenti*, *Divertimento* for string orchestra, *Concerto for Two Pianos and Orchestra*, *Contradizione* for chamber orchestra, *In una parte* for orchestra, the *Viola Concerto*, and *Four Caprices* for solo violin. In 1969 she was working on another ballet, *Pożądanie* (*Desire*), but she never got to finish it.

The prevailing style of socialist realism

In 1960 Grażyna Bacewicz's daughter, Alina Biernacka, completed her first year of studies at the Academy of Fine Arts in Warsaw. Her work was exhibited at the annual exhibition of students' artwork, along with portraits painted by her friends for which she had been the model. This was a delightful event for the family.

In July 1960, following an invitation from Andrzej's sister, Jadwiga Ciccotti, Grażyna and Alina travelled to Italy. This was an important experience for a fine arts student. Among the places they visited in Venice were St Mark's Basilica, the Doge's Palace, the Scuola Grande di San Rocco (with its Tintoretto collection), the Church of Saint Sebastian (with its frescos and decoration by Veronese), and the Venice Biennale exhibition of international contemporary art and sculpture. In Rome they visited the Sistine Chapel, the Vatican Museum, and Saint Peter's Basilica. They also went to the cinema to see Federico Fellini's recent film, *La Dolce Vita*, which had just been awarded the Palme d'Or at the 1960 Cannes Film Festival. Andrzej's family also took them to Naples and Capri.

Grażyna, knowing that the letters that she sent from Italy to New York would not be censored, described to her brother the prevailing situation in Poland: 'I wanted to take the opportunity to tell you that things back home are currently worse than they were a year ago in every respect. For example, censorship is killing writers and journalists. At the Academy of Fine Arts, for example, they've announced that the prevailing style is socialist realism; but the youngsters are making fun of it and embracing abstractionism. They've even started interfering with us musicians. Obviously, it's not a return to Stalinism, but they're really putting the screws on. It's getting more difficult with travelling. It's become more difficult too with artists' earnings, as they "see to it" that we don't have too much. And from time to time, letters (those from abroad) get read.'[2]

Not long after she returned from the trip, Grażyna threw herself into a festival whirl. During the fourth Warsaw Autumn, on 19 September 1960, the first performance of her *String Quartet No. 6* took place. It was given by the Parrenin Quartet. 'My *Sixth Quartet*, which was played at the festival, upset some of the older ones (such as Kazimierz Sikorski),' she wrote to her brother. 'But it surprised the youngsters. This lot had thought that I wasn't able to move forward anymore, so then they gave me their approval again.

But it's just that you get to a point as a composer where in your music you absolutely have to get away from what was, as you've lost interest in everything in the old sense and you're searching for something entirely new in the music. The youngsters perhaps go a bit too weird (as is their right!), while the middle-aged ones do try to get some music into this "weirdness" – not just experimentation. Anyway, without the freedom to experiment, there's no progress. Despite everything, I've come out unscathed.'[2]

Stefan Kisielewski declared that 'In *Quartet No. 6*, Grażyna Bacewicz set herself the task of keeping all the movements of the piece in twelve-tone technique, while avoiding a hackneyed effect and staying true to herself. She has achieved her aim – for those interested, I heartily recommend that they study this interesting little score.'[9]

'What's going on in the head of a very tired composer'

In 1961 Bacewicz introduced the world to a new composition called *Pensieri notturni*. Its premiere took place in April 1961 in Italy, during the Venice Biennale, and it was performed by the Kraków Philharmonic Chamber Orchestra, conducted by Andrzej Markowski. The following year the piece received the Ministry of Culture and Art Award. Grażyna attended the rehearsals for its performance in Kraków. According to her own notes, the premise of the piece was: 'To present in an organized way, something that has in no way been organized; in other words, what's going on in the head of a very tired composer. And as such, the title *Pensieri* is not strictly accurate. On the surface, following this clarification, it might appear that this music is in some sense programmatic. But only on the surface. The sound material that I use in this piece is not based on any pre-existing system, but one that has been rigorously established by me. The one thing that is derivative is the non-repetition of sounds. The subject matter of the piece has forced me to treat the instruments in a specific way, particularly the strings.' [14]

About the causes of her tiredness, Grażyna wrote to her brother as follows: 'In a few days' time I'll be going to Kraków for a performance of that piece for chamber orchestra, but I'm very anxious about it. I've found it difficult to work recently, as I have a neighbour who either plays the accordion right up against my wall, or else whistles. It drives me mad.'[2]

One may wonder whether these difficult composing conditions might have inspired Grażyna to write her *Pensieri notturni* and to transfer her struggles with her noisy neighbour to paper. In 1964 she wrote a novella called *Oporny hydraulik* (*The Obstreperous Plumber*), which describes the problem of noise making it impossible for creative artists to do their work.

After years of separation

Around that time, in early 1961, Vytautas was making serious preparations for travel. The last time he had seen his family was before World War II. Now that he had legal status as an American citizen, following many years of application, a trip abroad was finally possible. To be able to meet up with his sisters and his sister-in-law in Western Europe, he had had to send his official invitation to Warsaw, get it certified beforehand by the Polish Consulate, and provide a guarantee of financial support for them. Wanda, bolstered by her first volume of poetry: *Cisza i ciemność* (*The Silence and the Dark*), which had been 'very nicely published' by Czytelnik (as Grażyna informed her brother), was making her first trip to the West.

Following a long exchange of letters, it was agreed that they would meet up in France. 'Should you arrive before us, there's this accommodation in Paris, the Hotel Laffitte on the Rue Laffitte near Boulevard Haussmann. It's an affordable hotel, and it's right in the city centre. Alinka and I don't like the *Quartier Latin*. In the summer, when there are no students around, it's sad there, not very welcoming', Grażyna wrote persuasively.[2]

A few days later, no doubt nervous about meeting up with the brother whom she hadn't seen in such a long time, she added: 'Boccaccio's *Decameron* has given me a thought. As all of us who are meeting up are mavericks, and it would be difficult to agree on a schedule for the day, I suggest that on each of the days, one of us (taking it in turn) be the "king" of the group who decides on that day's schedule. Then everyone is afforded the same opportunities. What do you say to that?'[2]

Everything was ready by the beginning of July. The women had their passports and their French visas, as well as their transit visas for Belgium and Germany (East and West). On 20 July 1961, following many years of separation, the family finally met up in Le Havre. They had an unforgettable time in Paris.

On her return to Warsaw, Grażyna wrote: 'Dear Witek! Once again, many, many thanks for everything. Now that I've got to know you again, you've become even more close and dear to me, and I must say that I have such admiration for you, as you're even able to regard yourself in an objective way, never mind others.'[2] A week later, Grażyna added the following information: 'I'm going to start composing in October. The festival starts on the sixteenth and continues till the twenty-fourth. Of my pieces they'll be playing the eight-minute-long piece for chamber orchestra, *Pensieri notturni*.'[2]

'Which platform for the train to Petersburg?'

The year 1962 got off to a brisk start. Grażyna wrote to her brother: 'Today [12 January] they're playing my *Music for Strings, Trumpets and Percussion* in the

Philharmonic, with Rowicki conducting, giving it some real throttle. Soon after he'll be going to Amsterdam and conducting it there on the twenty-fourth. The record won't be ready for another half-year. Production takes ages here!'[2]

In April Grażyna was invited for a second time to be a member of the jury at the Tchaikovsky Competition in Moscow. She went to the competition with Alina. 'We all went to a concert,' she wrote to Wanda, 'where we heard Shostakovich's *Symphony No. 4*, which, being a formalist one, hadn't been played for 25 years. An interesting piece. Very well received by the audience.'[2] Mother and daughter attended numerous official meetings and receptions and met many outstanding musicians, such as Joseph Szigeti, Efrem Zimbalist, Gregor Piatigorsky, Dmitri Shostakovich, George Georgescu, Leonid Kogan, Karel Pravoslav Sádlo, Maurice Maréchal, and Harry Neuhaus. They also went to visit David Oistrakh, and, of course, wrote home very meticulously about everything.

Between the first and the second rounds of the competition, Grażyna and Alina travelled to Leningrad to see the collection of paintings at the Hermitage Museum, which were, as they told their family, 'exclusively foreign paintings – not Russian ones. Of Rembrandts alone, for example, there are a dozen or so, plus a Picasso gallery, a few Matisses, a Gauguin gallery, and so on. (Lots of French painters!)'[2]

During this escapade, when they were on their way to the renamed city, Grażyna made a funny mistake: 'I don't know what came over me – a mental block – and I asked: "What platform for the train to Petersburg?"' she wrote home. She then summed up this short visit to Leningrad: 'A beautiful city, but we were unlucky with the weather. It rained incessantly, and they have strange mud over there, so that straight away, your feet seem to have been dipped in black ink.'[2]

That same year, on 17 September 1962, at the Sixth Warsaw Autumn, Grażyna Bacewicz's *Concerto for Large Symphony Orchestra* had its premiere. It was played by the National Philharmonic Orchestra and conducted by Witold Rowicki, to whom the piece had been dedicated.

Stefan Kisielewski maintained that 'this piece is impressive precisely because it combines the fundamental characteristics of Grażyna's musical personality with a modernized technique. Where will this road lead her? We hear that she's lying low and secretly preparing her *Cello Concerto No. 2*.'[9]

'I'll keep pushing ahead'

After the Warsaw Autumn of 1962 had ended, Grażyna Bacewicz indirectly, in the form of advice, revealed to her brother her thoughts on the prevailing musical trends: 'In Europe, it's mainly the youngsters whose music gets played. So you should compose a piece that is not too long, for example, a piece in one movement for a very unusual group (chamber orchestra) – a dozen or so people or even fewer! It's mainly those kinds of pieces that they take an interest in at the festivals (the spirit of the times!). Oh, and the music would have to be very weird. Something that we haven't had yet. Obviously there are lots of daft things being produced by composers right now, but there are also very many interesting things. One thing's for sure, that in some way we have to tear ourselves away from our old way of musical thinking. That's what I think, and I'm personally never going to go back to compositions like, for example, *Quartet No. 4* (the one that won) or *Piano Études*, because I now find them boring. Obviously, I'm too old to completely tear myself away from my old music, even if I wanted to, but I'll keep pushing ahead, while I have the strength.'[2]

'They play "background music" upstairs'

In the autumn of 1962 Grażyna Bacewicz's daughter, Alina, married the artist Jerzy Sendłak, whom she had met a few years earlier at the Academy of Fine Arts. They celebrated with a select group of twelve people at the apartment in Koszykowa Street.

After this, Grażyna decided to swap the apartment for two smaller ones. It had not been an easy decision to make. What had tipped the balance was the fact that Andrzej's health had taken a serious turn for the worse, which now made it impossible for him to carry on with his private medical practice.

So, the family began packing and making plans for renovation. The old life on Koszykowa Street began slipping away, slowly disappearing, turning into memories. The apartment that had survived wartime airstrikes would soon be empty. New paint would silence the sound of the pieces composed therein. Grażyna wrote to Vytautas: 'Our application to change our one apartment for two has gone well. There are still some official matters, the refurbishment, the move, and so on. Enough to make my skin crawl, but we'll just have to put up with it. It's good that Andrzej has gone off to the sanatorium, as he'll avoid all this mess. He quite likes it there; we're in regular contact.'[2]

At the beginning of December 1962, Grażyna made a permanent move to her new apartment at 4 Mochnackiego Street. She wrote enthusiastically to Kiejstut and Halszka: 'My dears! We've settled in now. On Friday, Andrzej's nameday, we had fourteen medics here (and us five). As I'd bought the children a ping-pong table, we ate off it, and it looked quite impressive. I'm beginning to get used to this apartment. The drawbacks: upstairs they play "background music"; between 1.30 and 2 a.m. the milk gets delivered to the shop, so it's noisy; between 7.30 and 8 a.m. they take the garbage away, so more noise. The sleep situation is lousy. I don't know what it's like for Andrzej with his room at the back. I expect he gets noise when the cars drive off. It's been warm up until now. The only new things I've bought are curtains, a full wall's width, for Andrzej's room, and a lounge chair, because he was complaining about it being uncomfortable for him to write at his desk while sitting in the armchair. Jurek [Jerzy] has made some modern curtain rods for the curtains (we've bought some wood and some panes of glass). My room is bigger than the other one, so it's more comfortable, but I haven't got round to composing yet. I am tired.'[2]

'Should the earth spin off its axis'

From the beginning of 1963, Andrzej's illness continued to worsen. Taken up with caring for her husband, Grażyna had little time for creative work. She exchanged many letters at the time with Vytautas, in which she advised him on compositional matters. One day she gave away her secret: 'I've worked out a "little system" for myself (Kiej doesn't know anything about it) which comes out of serialism and depends on my never using any repeated consecutive notes either in a line of music or in the chords arising from it. It's a kind of loose serialism. As a result, you'll never find doubled-up notes in any of the chords. I am aware that this is in fact a 'little system' relating solely to the harmony, but that's fine, because as a result, I've finally moved away from tonality. It generates some very interesting harmonic effects. In this way all the notes are "working" constantly. It's entered my blood now, to the extent that I'm forever checking, if I'm constructing something multi-layered, what notes are available, and I only use those. And it always sounds good. Should the earth spin off its axis, I wouldn't allow myself to use a note that's already there. I'm sticking to that, for the time being.'[2]

In March 1963 Andrzej was back in hospital. During the day, Grażyna spent many hours by his bedside. She described one such day in a letter to Wanda: 'I had dinner today at the hospital, and now I'm there writing little letters at the desk, while Andrzej's snoring. He can now get from the bed to the desk by himself, and today he's also been out on the balcony in his wheelchair. I often slip out of the hospital for coffee and cake, but generally, when Andrzej's doing better, I don't stay for too long (in total around seven and a half hours). I always find some errand to run, so don't worry about me.'[2]

In the same period, maybe while in the hospital, Grażyna wrote a letter to Vytautas, in which she passed on some musical tips to him (although repeating a few points she had made in an earlier letter) and also her concern about the forthcoming festival: 'Taking into consideration the practical side of our composing life, I'd say write something shorter (a slick overture, or something of the kind), as it's easier for someone to shove a shorter piece into a programme. It's much more difficult with symphonies. I know that conductors are always on the lookout for striking short works, up to ten minutes. Have a think about it. I'm also intending to write a one-movement piece of this kind after the holidays.

'Our annual festival has a question mark hanging over it for two reasons: 1. The Government has to make savings (a harsh winter, a difficult economic situation, as in many countries). 2. Our great neighbour has voiced its opposition to the new currents in art. The Composers' Union is still trying to haggle over the festival, albeit a slimmed-down version, but we don't know what will be the outcome of these attempts.'[2]

During this difficult period, on returning home, Grażyna still sat down to compose, probably at night time. From the letters that she wrote at the time to her brother, we find that she was working on her *Cello Concerto No. 2*, which she was preparing specially for the coming Seventh Warsaw Autumn. The performer was to be the famous Spanish virtuoso, Gaspar Cassadó.

The piece was composed at a time when Grażyna was leaning towards sonorism in her musical creations. Here then, sonoristic elements, imbued with the composer's individuality, meet with motifs and traditional ways of structuring a piece.

Two months went by before the concerto was finished; from Grażyna's letter to Vytautas, we know that this was in May 1963: 'I've finally got to the end of my concerto, but I still have to write out the score (third movement), the instrumental parts (third movement), write out two copies, and three copies of the instrumental and cello parts. As Cassadó has gone quiet, even though he's had two of the movements for ages, I suspect that musically it's too strange for him, and that he doesn't know what to do. So, to be on the safe side, I've got in touch with Wiłkomirski, but it might be too difficult or weird for him as well. To be honest, the best cellists are in Russia, but they wouldn't do a premiere. So, the concerto could be a disaster. Well, we'll see.'[2]

Saying goodbye to her husband

Between May and July 1963, there was a marked deterioration in the health of Andrzej. Grażyna, on the edge of endurance, wrote to her brother on 5 July 1963: 'The care he's getting is wonderful. He'd not have that anywhere else in the world. Every day he gets seen by a whole crowd of doctors, in addition to the three permanent ones; and the nurses and orderlies are very caring. If they could do anything for him to help him in his illness, they absolutely would.'[2]

Three weeks later, Grażyna explained: 'I haven't written for a while because I can't really write. It's not to do with the time, but with the fact that with Andrzej it's a case of two days worse, two days better, over and over again – a kind of seesaw – so before this letter reaches you, things will be quite different. The doctors are about to "throw me out" of the hospital. But don't worry about me at all, as I am eating, and I am sleeping a bit, and I'm outdoors a lot, as I walk to the hospital.'[2]

Professor Andrzej Biernacki died on 30 July 1963. He was buried on 2 August at the Military Cemetery in Warsaw. Grażyna wrote to her brother: 'There were a few hundred people – around a thousand at the funeral; doctors carried his coffin on their shoulders for one and a half kilometres; there were five speeches. Masses of wreaths and flowers; there were very many announcements and obituaries in the newspapers, and articles from assorted institutions; and from us too; and on the radio, and programmes on television. They're about to publish two of my thank-yous for the care that Andrzej received and for the compassion shown.'[2]

9 A Final Creative Outpouring

Cellos soothe sorrow

In the autumn of 1963, Grażyna returned to composing. Only her work could comfort her and divert her thoughts from her painful memories. 'I feel all right. I've started a bit of work – I've started my *Quartet* for four cellos. The festival concert where my *Cello Concerto* is going to be played won't be conducted by Rowicki, but by another conductor, Krzemieński. I'm a bit worried about whether it'll be all right,' she wrote to her brother.[2]

On the opening day of the festival, the *Concerto* still wasn't ready for performance, which greatly worried Grażyna. She described the situation to Vytautas: 'A mad race and all sorts of responsibilities. I'm a bit concerned, as Cassadó only arrives on the evening of the twenty-seventh (he's playing on the twenty-ninth), so he'll only have two rehearsals. The orchestra's already working on it, but it's been written in such a way that without the cello part, which is the thread that ties all the music into some kind of sense, the orchestral players don't understand anything that's going on. I hadn't expected it to be so very strange, and I don't know whether Cassadó, who hasn't played much modern music in his life, won't get lost, when he hears what's happening in the orchestra, because his part is relatively normal.'[2]

The premiere of Grażyna Bacewicz's *Cello Concerto No. 2* took place at the end of the seventh Warsaw Autumn on 29 September 1963. Gaspard Cassadó was the soloist, and the orchestra was the National Philharmonic, with Witold Krzemieński conducting.

By the middle of November 1963, the *Quartet* for four cellos was ready. It had taken Grażyna Bacewicz two and a half months to compose this piece. Its premiere took place at the following Warsaw Autumn, on 24 September 1964. The composer wrote the following programme note: 'I was drawn to the four-cello combination through the richness of its sound properties. While working on this composition, I came to the conclusion that an ensemble of four cellos is an inexhaustible treasure for the contemporary composer. My concept of the piece forced me to reject, to a considerable degree, certain elements that are perhaps most characteristic of cello-playing, e.g., a broad *cantilena*. I will probably return to this line-up and treat it entirely differently. The *Quartet* for four cellos consists of two movements entitled: 1. "Narrazione"; 2. "Riflessioni".'[15]

From Mademoiselle Boulanger to Maestro Stravinsky

At the beginning of April 1964, before Easter, Nadia Boulanger came to Poland to take part in the performance of a composition by her sister Lili. Grażyna organized various meetings for her, and invited her home for Easter, to meet family and friends. Both composers also attended a reception at the French Embassy. Grażyna wrote to Vytautas: 'She's an old woman, but never tired and always full of energy. It's scary!'[2]

After Nadia Boulanger's departure, Grażyna left for Kraków for the premiere of her cantata *Akropolis* for mixed choir and orchestra. The piece was written for the six hundredth anniversary of Kraków's Jagiellonian University. The concert took place on 10 May 1964 with Andrzej Markowski conducting the Kraków Philharmonic Orchestra.

After the concerts of the eighth Warsaw Autumn were over, Grażyna celebrated the premiere of her *Quartet* for four cellos, together with the Lutosławskis and Michał Spisak and his wife. Grażyna may well have sensed that this would be the last time that she would be seeing her friend; it was no secret that Michał Spisak was seriously ill.

In October, on behalf of the Union of Polish Composers, Grażyna Bacewicz went to Yugoslavia, together with her daughter. 'What we liked most was the mosques and the old town in Sarajevo,' she wrote to Vytautas, 'as it's very exotic, and we both like that, and also the bus journey from Sarajevo to Mostar. Very beautiful scenery (rivers, mountains). Belgrade, though a large city is nothing special. I was in touch with the Composers' Union – I had to listen to a lot of their music on tape; there was a reception, an interview, and so on. You know what it's like on that kind of trip. On the eighteenth, four of us are going up to Poznań. What they'll do on stage will be a surprise to me, as I don't want to go up earlier for the rehearsals, but the conductor there is very devoted to me, the opera director, so I think they'll make an effort.'[2]

In mentioning the journey to Poznań, Grażyna is referring to her trip to attend the premiere of her one-act ballet, *Esik in Ostend*. The libretto was written by Lech Terpiłowski, based on a poem by Tadeusz Boy-Żeleński. The choreography and production were by Conrad Drzewiecki, while Stanisław Bąkowski created the stage design. When the curtain went up at the Poznań Opera on 18 October 1964, the orchestra played under the baton of Robert Satanowski.

The family spent Christmas and New Year in Krynica. 'We're sitting like idiots in a café – bad coffee, and we're waiting for Kiej,' Grażyna informed Vytautas. 'It's cold in the villa. We can only get warm by telling each other jokes and thinking about you. All the very, very best to you, my dear!'[2]

On 29 January 1965 Grażyna received news that her long-time friend, Michał Spisak, had died. She could still remember her first stay to Paris, in the year 1938, and the time she spent there with a group of wonderful composer friends, amongst whom there was always Spisak. In February she wrote to her brother: 'Thank you very much for the nameday wishes!!! And so, the year skips by again. Have you written to Andrée Spisak following Michał's death? Fortunately, the Rowickis just happened to be in Paris, so they helped her with the funeral.'[2]

Life carried on, but the number of people who were close to Grażyna was gradually shrinking.

The new apartment on Mochnackiego Street was bright and comfortable. Grażyna often played host to her daughter Alina and son-in-law Jerzy, and their friends from the Academy of Fine Arts. Then the regular sound of a ping-pong ball would often mark time in the afternoons. In the composer's room, a smallish piano stood by the window, and beyond that, a small desk; on the other side there was a narrow day-bed. As soon as she managed to carve out some time for herself between the numerous meetings she had at the Polish Composers' Union, this was where she would shut herself up. Before composing, she would draw the floor-length curtains with an energetic pull and sit down at the piano. Then time would stand still, turning into notes and into pauses.

The whole of 1965 turned out to be an incredibly fruitful year for the composer. What contributed to this huge creative explosion? Maybe, with the major family tragedies of the last few years gradually having receded into memory, she had found space for creative thought. Grażyna spent nearly the entire year living alone. In December, her sister Wanda moved in. She was feeling ill, and she preferred to stay with Grażyna – which turned out to be a permanent arrangement.

In May 1965, Grażyna's daughter Alina had fifteen paintings ready and had just finished writing her dissertation at the Academy of Fine Arts. In the meantime, Grażyna had unexpectedly ended up in hospital, where she had an operation to have her appendix removed. It may be hard to believe, but ten days later she was involved in making a record: 'I'm currently recording an album. Well not so much me, as my compositions. Rowicki's conducting. The whole record's going to be mine. But it's a hell of a lot of work, especially as I'm madly trying to finish and correct one of the pieces, as Zakład Nagrań [the recording label] wanted more recent pieces. Of the old ones there's going to be one short *Overture*,' she told Vytautas in a letter.[2]

And then, at the end of May, there was an important guest, as she also informed her brother: 'I feel fine now. Stravinsky's come to Warsaw, so there's a bit of dancing attendance around him. He came to see us at the Composers' Union. The mood got very warm and friendly. We know that he can be unpleasant on occasion, so that just shows how well it went.'[2]

Musica sinfonica in tre movimenti and foot-stamping applause

In her new composition entitled *Musica sinfonica in tre movimenti*, Grażyna Bacewicz moved away from the four-movement symphonic convention. She wrote enigmatic and sombre music, in which dark, tension-creating colours can be heard. In her musical narrative, she abandoned longer phrasing and an explicit relationship between consecutive sequences. The way she structured the three movements, *Tesi – Dialogo – Gioco*, was to state the themes in the first movement, develop conversations between them in the second, and let them play themselves out in the final movement.

After a holiday in Ustka, Grażyna travelled to Sweden for the premiere of the piece. This took place in Stockholm on 6 September 1965, with the National Philharmonic Orchestra performing and Witold Rowicki conducting. In her notes, Grażyna wrote that she had not planned to write this composition for any specific festival, but that when Rowicki saw the score, he immediately suggested that it be performed both in Stockholm (at a concert of contemporary Polish music) and at the Warsaw Autumn.

Of the first performance she wrote: 'In Stockholm, although there's only a small group of people interested in new music, the Polish music met with a lot of success. They have a custom there of stamping their feet as they clap, if they like a composition. And after my composition, and others too, there was much stamping on the floor.'[8]

In October 1965, after the ninth Warsaw Autumn had ended, Grażyna went on a business trip to Bucharest for the Congress of Executive Committees of Composers' Unions.

In 1965 Grażyna also composed her *Little Triptych* for piano, dedicated to the pianist Regina Smendzianka, who performed its premiere in Helsinki. She also worked on one of her important chamber works, her *String Quartet No. 7*; however, she decided that the version that she was working on that year (1965) was unsatisfactory, so she returned to the composition the following year. She also wrote her *Divertimento* for string orchestra, which had been commissioned by Karol Teutsch, who conducted its premiere with the National Philharmonic Chamber Orchestra in Munich on 21 November 1966.

Some of the pieces that Grażyna Bacewicz composed during this period were only premiered after the composer's death. This is the case with *Incrustations* for horn and chamber orchestra, which had its first performance in 1972 in Wrocław; the *Trio* for oboe, harp, and percussion, which was first performed on 2 June 1974 in Bennington, Vermont, in the USA; and also the *Piano Quintet No. 2*, which had its premiere in May 1972 in Salzburg. The last, dedicated to the Warsaw Piano Quintet – in other words, violinists Igor Iwanow and Jan Tawroszewicz, viola player Stefan Kamasa, cellist Andrzej Orkisz, and pianist Władysław Szpilman – and written thirteen years after *Quintet No. 1*, shows a significant change in the composer's creative aesthetic.

Bacewicz was searching for a new form of expression, new tone colour. She was interested in the avant-garde, in twelve-note technique, and in aleatoricism (the use of chance). She introduced impressionistic sound effects, which she achieved through short phrases and motifs passed around among the instruments, but she based the structure of the *Quintet No. 2* on classical forms.

Violin Concerto No. 7 and String Quartet No. 7

The three-movement *Violin Concerto No. 7*, an exceptionally virtuosic composition, with a clear structure and outer movements in sonata-allegro form, brought Grażyna Bacewicz a Belgian Government prize and a gold medal in the international Queen Elisabeth Competition in Brussels. Agustín Léon Ara, to whom the composition had been dedicated, performed the concerto on 14 January 1966, with the Belgian Radio and Television Symphony Orchestra, and Daniel Sternefeld conducting.

'The performer wrote Grażyna a lovely letter,' we read in Wanda's letter to Vytautas, 'saying that as he was learning the concerto, he kept wondering who could have written such beautiful music, so brilliantly written for violin, and he sent her some excellent reviews. Because over there, during the final, they play a piece with orchestra – at that point still under wraps. Grażyna got the message about the prize after the event, in other words, after the final ceremony, but, in any case, these days she wouldn't have gone. She prefers to work.'[2] Indeed, the composer had not been present in the concert hall when the prizes had been announced; she had, however, had a premonition relating to the date when they were awarded: one night she had dreamed about a tram moving along a road with an exceptionally clear number '14'.

So, the year 1966 had begun with a bang.

Grażyna would soon be starting work on some significant compositions: her *Concerto for Two Pianos and Orchestra* and her *Contradizione* for chamber orchestra. For the time being, however, as we learn from her letters, she was still working on her *Quartet No. 7*: 'Right now, Wanda's with some children, and she's posing for them, in other words, she's being a model (but not a nude one). I'm reworking my *Quartet No. 7*, which I ruined, or rather didn't do very well in its first version. I hate reworking. My *Quartet No. 7* hasn't, of course, been printed yet, as it's yet to have its first performance. It might be performed in September in Warsaw at the festival.'[2]

The piece was, however, played much earlier than the composer had anticipated – on 15 May 1966, in Łańcut. 'The premiere of my *Quartet No. 7* went rather well,' she informed Vytautas. 'In the palace near Rzeszów they have these Chamber Music Days and Dimov's quartet from Bulgaria played. They're also going to be playing (mine as well) at the Warsaw Autumn. My piece for organ hasn't turned out well. I met up again with that French organist, and he very politely told me about the finer points: for example, the impossibility of changing register while playing. That taught me a thing or two, but I'd have to get to know the instrument better, to be able to write something for it.'[2]

That particular piece for organ was *Esquisse*, and the French organist in question was Jean Guillou, to whom Grażyna Bacewicz had dedicated the composition. It was Guillou too who, after the composer's death, performed the premiere of this three-minute-long piece on 8 June 1969 in Bordeaux.

In June 1966 Grażyna Bacewicz was looking forward to the birth of her granddaughter. She also made an important professional decision: 'I have agreed to teach composition at the Higher School of Music in Warsaw, as they've given me very good terms. I'm only going to be teaching six hours per week, plus the occasional meeting,' she wrote to her brother.[2]

At the end of June, Alina gave birth to a little girl: Joanna. Grażyna and Wanda were absolutely thrilled. That summer, the sisters, who had preferred to stay put in Warsaw to be on hand all the time, should any help be needed with the granddaughter, decided to sign up for a course of driving lessons. Once they had passed the required state exam on the construction of a car engine and on road regulations, they just needed to take their driving tests. However, due to concerns over a stern examiner, they decided to take the test after the autumn festival. That year the audience at the tenth Warsaw Autumn was able to hear Grażyna Bacewicz's *Quartet No. 7*.

'It went well,' wrote the composer to her brother. 'Amazingly, they're even writing good things about it. The *Violin Concerto* (the one that won a prize) I didn't want to have played at the festival, as it wouldn't have been right for this event. I preferred to give them my *Quartet*.'[2]

At the start of the new academic year 1966/1967, Grażyna Bacewicz took over the composition class at the State Higher School of Music in Warsaw. Once she had settled down in her new role, she wrote to Vytautas: 'I have three students; two Poles and one Yugoslavian [Dubravko Detoni], who graduated in composition in Belgrade. The Polish boys have only just started at the upper school (they've studied all the theoretical subjects at the intermediate school), but they're going to be doing counterpoint again at the upper school, and suchlike, but not with me. I'm teaching them composition, instrumentation, and score reading.'[2]

Despite her numerous commitments, Grażyna Bacewicz also managed to compose her planned *Concerto for Two Pianos* (although audiences had to wait well over a year for it to be premiered) and finish work on her chamber orchestra piece *Contradizione*, which had been commissioned by the Hopkins Center for the Arts in the US. 'My choice of instruments wasn't incidental; in fact, it was the fundamental issue. The juxtaposition of all kinds of musical contradictions (like, for instance, ways of playing that "don't go together well") had to be dependent on the instruments in the piece,' wrote the composer. 'Obviously the juxtaposition of contradictions was not an end in itself. The overriding aim was to create a piece out of these contradictory elements that would not only "withstand" these musical contradictions but would also (as a result of its construction) be able to bind them together so tightly as to make them produce a fresh aesthetic experience as a result.'[16]

Contradizione had its premiere on 16 July 1967 in the United States, as part of the Summer Festival of Contemporary Music in Hanover, New Hampshire. It was conducted by Mario di Bonaventura.

'My music is not meant for rousing sleepyheads'

Since giving up smoking in mid-September 1966, Grażyna found that her work was not proceeding as fast as it had done previously. But she bravely stuck to her resolution, and on 3 July 1967, she assured her brother that for nearly ten months not a single cigarette had touched her lips! She was working at the time on her *Concerto for Viola and Orchestra*, which she had promised Stefan Kamasa. However, she unexpectedly broke off this work.

She wrote about this to her family: 'Kamasa's going to weep, as I'm putting his *Concerto* aside. My plans have altered. I have to write an orchestral piece for Cuzán for that festival in February in Havana. I need to have handed in the score by the beginning of December. The trip to Cuba (the flight alone) takes eighteen hours, and the whole trip (as there are three stopovers) – about 24 hours. I'll be there for about three weeks. (If I wanted to, I could stay longer.) There's also an orchestra going with us, with two conductors – probably Markowski and Czyż – and two more composers (but my music's going to be played by the local orchestra with Cuzán). A pity I'll not be on my own. That's a place I'd prefer to be on my own. However, I'm dismayed by all that England business in July. Maybe I'll be able to get out of going. They told me today in Ars Polonie that they've had to send them another five *Pensieri* scores, in other words, they've gone completely daft over that piece. Well, anyway, I'm going to have to "think up" something very strong for Cuba. But how? I just can't compose anymore. So, instead of composing, I've been sewing.'[2]

Grażyna did not, in the end, go to Cuba, but her orchestral piece *In una parte* (which had been commissioned by the organizers of the International Festival of Contemporary Music in Havana) did have its premiere on 2 October 1968, with the National Orchestra of Cuba conducted by Manuel Duchesne Cuzán. On the other hand, Grażyna did travel to England in July 1967 to the Cheltenham Music Festival, during which the BBC Northern Symphony Orchestra, conducted by George Hurst, performed her *Pensieri notturni*.

Grażyna spent part of August 1967 in the village of Urle, with her daughter and granddaughter. 'Joasia's a bolt of lightning, not a human being, so you get the idea,' she wrote to her brother.[2] After a brief period of questionable rest, she returned to intense activity.

In September 1967 Grażyna Bacewicz was given the title of 'Professor of Music', and in October 1967, as she did every year, she took part in the Warsaw Autumn. 'I don't really have anything to tell you about the Warsaw Festival. My piece didn't make much of an impact. The first concert isn't good, as you have a special audience and people haven't woken up yet, and my music is not meant for rousing sleepyheads,' she wrote after her *Contradizione* was performed at the opening.[2]

Shortly afterwards, Grażyna Bacewicz was made chair of the jury for the fifth International Henryk Wieniawski Violin Competition, which took place in Poznań between 4 and 19 November 1967. Amongst the jury members were Irena Dubiska, Eugenia Umińska, Tadeusz Wroński, Henryk Szeryng, Jean Fournier, Henri Gagnebin, Remy Prìncipe, and Emil Kamiliarov. The winner was a sixteen-year-old pupil of Irena Dubiska: Piotr Janowski; second place went to the Russian, Mikhail Bezverkhny; and third went to the eighteen-year-old Kaja Danczowska. The competition's opening concert featured a performance by Konstanty Andrzej Kulka.

'Though it's already nearly 1 a.m.,' Grażyna wrote to her sister, 'I'll just tell you about Kulka. Well, his playing exceeded all my expectations. Completely as if someone had just dropped down from heaven. Everything he plays, he plays supremely well. He really is a phenomenon. He plays without any stage fright. The camera people from the television behaved like barbarians. Any other soloist would have lost it by the second bar; they were moving around with the camera, making a terrible noise, right under his nose, in front of the front row (so, under my nose too); their shoes squeaking; in a word: a scandal – and he didn't bat an eyelid.'[2]

While the competition was still ongoing, Grażyna, with the help of her sister Wanda, was dealing with the necessary formalities for her next trip. She was due to leave for Naples at the beginning of December 1967, where she was to be a jury member at the Alberto Curci Violin Competition. She told Halszka and Kiejstut about the imminent trip: 'I'm going to Naples on Friday (by train), and so I'll not be around for fifteen, sixteen days. I've been invited to be on the jury of a violin competition, but I will switch off from the sounds. I'm going because I like Italy.'[2]

In the shadow of the March events

The *Viola Concerto* that she had started composing earlier was finished by Grażyna Bacewicz in 1968. Stefan Kamasa eventually performed it on 20 June 1969 in Warsaw, with the National Philharmonic Orchestra conducted by Witold Rowicki. During gaps while working on the concerto, Grażyna wrote her *Four Caprices* for solo violin, and a song, *Courtship* (after Adam Mickiewicz) for unaccompanied male-voice choir.

On 15 March 1968 Grażyna Bacewicz's *Concerto for Two Pianos and Orchestra*, which she had written two years earlier, had its premiere. It was performed by the National Philharmonic Orchestra, under the baton of Witold Rowicki, with Jerzy Maksymiuk and Jerzy Witkowski playing the piano parts with great gusto, particularly the piece's two extremely lively outer movements. The two piano parts were given equal weight and were both independent of each other and complementary in their musical discourse. The composer made sure, however, that the performers did not take too fast a tempo. After one of the rehearsals, standing in the wings, she opened her handbag, took out a small piece of paper and quickly wrote a little note to the conductor: 'Witek! Kissing your hand, I beg you – take it at a steadier pace: the whole beginning of the first movement (including the boys' entry) and the end of the third movement.'[8]

In March 1968 fighting broke out on the streets of Warsaw. Over two thousand uniformed and civilian officials were brought in to pacify the protesting students at the University of Warsaw. Stefan Kisielewski, who famously wrote the sentence about 'the scandalous dictatorship of philistines in Polish cultural life, that we have been seeing for quite some time,' was beaten up by 'unknown assailants'. The prevailing climate was difficult to bear; the authorities had stirred up antisemitic propaganda. Such circumstances made it difficult to focus on creative work. This may be why Grażyna Bacewicz took to writing prose at the time. She wrote a crime novel: *Sidła* (*Snares*), which was published by PWM in 2018.

Meanwhile in June 1968, Grażyna received news from the team at Teatr Telewizyjny (Television Theatre) that they had produced her dramatic piece *Jerzyki, albo nie jestem ptakiem* (*Martins, or I'm not a Bird*; originally called *To the Power of 2 and then some!*), which had been highly commended in the Ateneum theatre competition in 1963. It was produced by Edward Dziewoński, who also played the lead part. Grażyna described the congenial circumstances to her family: 'First of all Kobuszewski* thanked me for the flowers (he reminded me that he'd played King Arthur in the television version). He was very nice, and he "informed" me that they'd done the recording. Today Dziewoński rang in the same spirit, in other words, he was very nice. They are completely different. Kobuszewski is unsophisticated and rather shy. Dziewoński always puts on a bit of an act – as if he's got used to listening to his own fine-sounding voice.'[2]

In July 1968 Grażyna started work on her ballet *Desire*, with a libretto written by Mieczysław Bibrowski, based on a play by Pablo Picasso: *Desire Caught*

---

* Translator's note: Jan Kobuszewski (1934–2019) was an extremely popular, award-winning film, TV, and theatre actor, satirist, cabaret artist, and theatre director.

by the Tail. She spent the whole of July 1968 at home on her own, as her three 'ladies' had left for Zakopane.

'I've been sleeping a lot, so that I'm able to work. I start my work at 10 a.m. and finish at 10 p.m. Obviously with breaks throughout the day,' she reassured her sister in a letter, and then on 22 July she informed her brother: 'I popped up to Szczecin for the day (two nights in the train) as there was a competition there for a piece for organ, and I was one of the jurors. It tired me out a bit, as there were twenty-seven of these works and we had to gallop through it all within one day'.[2] (The jury awarded first prize to Henryk Mikołaj Górecki for his organ *Cantata*.) Once she had slipped this letter into an envelope, she reached for a fresh sheet of paper and wrote to Zakopane: 'Today, at midday, when they started shooting, I finished writing Scene I of Act II, and I've had enough for now. And shortly (it's 4 p.m.) Bibrowski will be coming... He wanted to boast about having spoken to Axer, whom we might be able to get to work with us.* He's apparently looking for a way of getting it staged throughout the world (as the Warsaw opera might mess it up after all, but even if not, it's still worth trying)'.[2]

In September 1968 Grażyna travelled to Budapest to fulfil her role of jury member in a String Quartet Competition. In October 1968, she decided against going to Cuba for the premiere of *In una parte*. Nine days after it had its premiere in Havana, the piece was performed for a second time, this time in Szczecin, under the direction of Renard Czajkowski.

'I'm going to be more choosy with my trips'

Grażyna's work on the ballet was going slowly. Before Christmas 1968, as planned, she set off to Armenia with a representation of Polish composers and musicians for the Decade of Polish Music. There she heard yet another performance of her *Concerto for Two Pianos and Orchestra* with Jerzy Maksymiuk and Jerzy Witkowski on piano and, on this occasion, Andrzej Markowski conducting.

Grażyna returned from Yerevan on 15 December 1968. It had been decided that the family's Christmas festivities would, that year, be taking place in the apartment on Mochnackiego Street. Wanda was having to deal with everything, as shortly after returning from her trip, Grażyna had fallen ill. On 20 December she sent a letter to Vytautas in America, worrying meanwhile about the late postal bottlenecks. 'As soon as I got back, I was laid up

---

* Mieczysław Bibrowski (1908–2000), who wrote the libretto to Bacewicz's ballet, *Desire*, was a lawyer, poet, journalist (French correspondent for Polish Press Agency), and screenwriter.
  Erwin Axer (1917–2012) was a theatre director, writer, and university professor.

with the flu. (I didn't actually stay in bed; I just didn't leave the house),' she wrote to her brother. 'I was worried that our building would go up in the air when I began sneezing. I know it's rude to sneeze loudly, but this was stronger than any considerations. The Kiejstuts are meant be coming to ours for Christmas. They were still being awkward about it up until three days ago, but I "explained to them" on the phone that we might die, after all, so it would be worth meeting up before then. (Obviously I know that we're going to stay alive a very long time; it was just my way of getting through to them.) My trip (3500 kilometres one way by plane) wasn't in any way interesting. It's taken up ten days of my life. I don't think I should put myself through that kind of thing anymore. I'm going to be more choosy with my trips now.'[2]

'Why are you writing about dying, Grażynko; are you feeling unwell?' Wanda was concerned.

'I was only joking,' Grażyna reassured her. However, she was not in a good way. At night-time, she felt sharp pains in her heart. The simplest of activities, such as washing the dishes or laying the table, took a lot out of her. They had a lovely time on Christmas Day, with Kiejstut in brilliant form playing Father Christmas; Grażyna's granddaughter Joasia remembered that day for many years to come

After the family left, the sisters welcomed in the New Year 1969 in the apartment on Mochnackiego Street.[17]

Though she was not feeling too well, Grażyna had no intention of taking it easy. There was going to be a concert of Tadeusz Baird's music at the Warsaw Philharmonic on 10 January 1969. Wanda was doubtful about her sister's evening plans.

'Grażynko, it's frightfully cold. There's a hard frost. Surely you're not going out in those little pumps?!'

'It's fine; it's nearby,' Grażyna cut her off as she left the apartment.

After the concert Grażyna Bacewicz felt unwell. A doctor was called for. He said she had the flu and prescribed antibiotics. A nurse came to the apartment to administer the injections. Grażyna was feeling increasingly unwell, but she continued to work, correcting the proofs of the short stories that she had written in recent years. She entitled the collection *Znak szczególny* (*A Distinguishing Mark*).

In the early hours of 17 January, Wanda called for an ambulance. The doctor said that Grażyna Bacewicz had had a heart attack. She was taken by ambulance to the Hospital of the Infant Jesus, the very clinic where her husband, Andrzej Biernacki, had worked all his life. She spent a few hours in the intensive care unit, but as her condition continued to deteriorate, she was taken to the resuscitation unit. When she momentarily regained consciousness, she whispered, barely audibly: 'Why have you woken me? It was so lovely...'

Grażyna Bacewicz died on 17 January 1969. She would have been sixty that February.

On 2 February 1969, Kiejstut wrote to Vytautas: 'Dearest Brother, There are only three of us left now. Fate has dealt us a terrible, unexpected blow; it has taken away one of our siblings, not the eldest of us, but the Being who meant so extraordinarily much to us in our family life (not to mention matters outside the family, general ones). Small wonder then that we are going around completely stunned spiritually, that we still can't understand what has happened, and that to our thoughts and feelings this parting is something frightfully alien. Grażynka carried a frightful amount on her shoulders, and now that she has departed, nothing can fill this void. She was so very much needed by both Alusia and Wandzia, and by all of us, her colleagues, her friends, and – as a creator – by the whole world. There was no-one as totally devoted to Grażyna as Wanda. As the whole city had fallen ill with flu, and people left, right, and centre were experiencing flu symptoms, along with a high temperature, it never entered any of our minds that Grażyna's state might have anything to do with heart disease. Even the doctor who was called out failed to identify it. Grażyna's system had been under strain for a long time and was worn out through overwork and constant worry.'[2]

To many people in the world of music, Grażyna Bacewicz's sudden departure came as a huge shock. Her funeral was held on 21 January 1969. Her coffin, decorated with wreaths, was put on display at the State Higher School of Music, and alongside, professors formed a guard of honour for many hours. Then the funeral cortège set off for the National Philharmonic. This is where the musical world said good-bye to the composer. Grażyna Bacewicz was laid to rest in the Alley of Distinguished Citizens at the Powązki Military Cemetery in Warsaw.

The manuscript score for her ballet *Desire* remained open on her piano. Grażyna had not finished the composition. On top of the sheet music lay a piece of paper with the composer's comments. The fragment of music needed to complete the score was added by the conductor and composer Bogusław Madey. The ballet's premiere took place on 18 March 1973 in the Wielki Theatre in Warsaw.

In 1983, a memorial plaque was set into the façade of the building at 35 Koszykowa Street, where Grażyna Bacewicz had lived and composed for twenty-six years: 'In this building, between the years 1936–1962 lived and composed Grażyna Bacewicz – a world-famous composer.'

'We all have our place in the world'

Grażyna Bacewicz is the composer of nearly two hundred works. Her musical style is very clear, just like the values she upheld. She often spoke of technique and form and the need for discipline while composing. She believed that music did not express so-called everyday emotions, but itself alone, its own purely musical emotions.

Keeping a close eye on the changes that were taking place in music, she experimented widely in her own compositions, for example in *String Quartet No. 6*, where she approached serialism. 'She did not, however, go down the road of serialism,' according to Stefan Kisielewski. 'Rather, her excursion into the territory of this technique helped her rid herself of the persistent residue of tonality and neoclassicism. She went the way of synthesis, continuing her somewhat bleak, very virile symphonic monumentalism. She furnished it with a number of elements from the new aesthetic, new textures and instrumental techniques.'[9]

This is what she wrote about her own creativity: 'As music is moving forward at a very rapid pace, thanks to young composers, I know that now I can only stand in the second row, because I can't surpass myself, and something genuinely new will be created by young composers, not by me. But I'm fine with that. We all have our place in the world.'[2]

Chronology of Life and Work

1909

5 February: Grażyna Bacewicz is born; a third child to Maria Modlińska and Vincas Bacevičius.

1916

26 June: Bacewicz siblings' first public concert in Braun's Hall at 64 Przędzalniana Street, Łódź.

1919

Grażyna starts attending the Janina Pryssewiczówna Private Girls' Humanities High School; she also attends the private music school of Helena Kijeńska and Antoni Dobkiewicz.

1923

Grażyna's father returns to Lithuania, crossing the border illegally; he spends the rest of his life in Kaunas.

1928

Grażyna begins studying at the State Music Conservatoire in Warsaw and at the University of Warsaw (Philosophy Department).

1930

First trip to Lithuania. Concerts at the Kaunas Conservatoire.

1932

Finishes her studies at Warsaw Conservatoire with two diplomas/degrees: violin and composition. Performs jointly with her brother, Vytautas, at concerts in Kaunas and Riga.

1932–1933
Studies in Paris with Nadia Boulanger (composition) and André Touret (violin).

1934
10 May: Warsaw Conservatoire puts on a Grażyna Bacewicz concert. The programme includes, amongst other pieces: *Children's Suite* and *Scherzo* for piano; *Stained Glass Window* and *Lithuanian Song* for violin and piano. Second trip to Paris to study with Carl Flesch.

1935
March: awarded a commendation in the first International Henryk Wieniawski Violin Competition in Warsaw.
September: joins the string section (principal first violin) of the Polish Radio Orchestra under Grzegorz Fitelberg (until 1938).

1936
March: *Trio* for oboe, violin, and cello commended in the Polish Music Publishers' Competition.
6 August: marries medical doctor, Andrzej Biernacki, at St Alexander's Church in Warsaw. The newly-weds set up home at number 35 Koszykowa Street.

1938
28 March: premiere of *Violin Concerto No. 1* with the composer as soloist, and the Polish Radio Orchestra conducted by Grzegorz Fitelberg.
November: goes to Paris, where she composes her *String Quartet No. 1*.

1939
26 April: concert of the composer's music at the École Normale de Musique; the programme includes *String Quartet No. 1*, *Sonata for Oboe and Piano*, and *Partita* for violin and piano.

1941
Plays her *Sonata* for solo violin at an underground concert in Warsaw.

1942
July: gives birth to a daughter, Alina, a future painter and poet.

1943
21 May: premiere of *String Quartet No. 2* by Eugenia Umińska's quartet at Bolesław Woytowicz's Art House café.
At a different concert, the *Suite for Two Violins* is premiered by Irena Dubiska and Eugenia Umińska.

1944

Spends the Warsaw Uprising in a shelter on Koszykowa Street.
After the suppression of the Warsaw Uprising, stays in Grodzisk Mazowiecki initially, then in Lublin.

1945

April–October: teaches violin and music theory at the Music Conservatoire in Łódź.
1 September: premiere of *Overture* in Kraków, with the Kraków Philharmonic Orchestra and Mieczysław Mierzejewski conducting.
November: returns to Warsaw to the apartment in 35 Koszykowa Street.

1946

Three-month tour of France, including performances at the Salle Pleyel (with the Orchestre Lamoureux and Paul Kletzki conducting), Salle Gaveau, and Salle YMCA.
18 October: premiere of *Violin Concerto No. 2* with the composer as soloist and the Łódź Philharmonic Orchestra, conducted by Tomasz Kiesewetter.

1947

9 May: recital at the École Normale de Musique in Paris; the programme includes *Sonata No. 2 for Violin and Piano*, with Jean Germain accompanying on piano.

1948

15 February: premiere of *Sonata No. 3 for Violin and Piano* with her brother, Kiejstut.
Olympic Cantata commended at the International Olympic Art Competition in London.

1949

4 March: Premiere in Gdańsk of *Violin Concerto No. 3*, performed by the composer with the Baltic Philharmonic under the baton of Stefan Śledziński.
April: awarded second prize for her *Piano Concerto* in the Fryderyk Chopin Composers' Competition.
November: awarded third prize in the second edition of the above competition for her *Concert Krakowiak*.

1950

Tour of Romania and Czechoslovakia; concert in Budapest.
18 June: premiere of *Concerto for String Orchestra* in Warsaw, with the WOSPR (Polish National Radio Symphony Orchestra) with Grzegorz Fitelberg conducting.

26 September: Grażyna and her brother Kiejstut perform the premiere of her *Sonata No. 4 for Violin and Piano*.

1951

October: awarded first prize in the International String Quartet Competition in Liège for her *String Quartet No. 4*, which the Quatuor Municipal de Liège had premiered on 21 September.
30 November–11 December: concerts in Belgium.
Awarded first prize at the first Festival of Polish Music for her *Sonata No. 4 for Violin and Piano*.

1952

Two premieres in Kraków with the Kraków Philharmonic Orchestra, conducted by Bohdan Wodiczko: 21 February – *Violin Concerto No. 4* (performed by the composer); 11 September – *Symphony No. 3*.
25 September–7 October: on the jury of the International String Quartet Competition in Liège; her *String Quartet No. 4* is one of the set pieces for competitors.
National Prize (second level) for *Violin Concerto No. 4*, *Sonata No. 4 for Violin and Piano*, and *String Quartet No. 4*.
December: on the jury of the second International Henryk Wieniawski Violin Competition in Poznań.
22 December: Grażyna's father dies in Kaunas.

1953

June: on the jury of the Long-Thibaud International Competition in Paris in both the violin and piano categories.

1954

15 January: premiere of *Symphony No. 4* in Kraków with Kraków Philharmonic Orchestra and Bohdan Wodiczko conducting.
25 July: premiere of her ballet *The Peasant King* at the Poznań Opera under the direction of Walerian Bierdiajew.
26 September: in a serious car accident; a long stay in hospital.
10 December: premiere in Kraków of *Polish Overture* with Kraków Philharmonic Orchestra, conducted by Bohdan Wodiczko.

1955

17 January: premiere of *Violin Concerto No. 5* at the second Festival of Polish Music, with Wanda Wiłkomirska as soloist, with the National Philharmonic Orchestra conducted by Witold Rowicki.
Festival prizes for: *Symphony No. 4*, *Violin Concerto No. 3*, and *String Quartet No. 3*.

1956

16 February–20 March: trip to India with Polish artistic delegation.
Wins second prize at the String Quartet Competition in Liège; visits Paris along the way.
First International Festival of Contemporary Music (later know as 'Warsaw Autumn'): performances of *Concerto for String Orchestra*, *Polish Overture*, and *String Quartet No. 4*.

1957

December: chair of the jury (which includes David Oistrakh, Irena Dubiska, Eugenia Umińska, and Yehudi Menuhin as honorary jury member) at the third International Henryk Wieniawski Violin Competition in Poznań.

1958

March and April: jury member (violin section) at the first International Tchaikovsky Violin Competition in Moscow.
June: delegate at the festival of the International Society for Contemporary Music in Strasbourg.
Second Warsaw Autumn: Regina Smendzianka gives premiere of the complete cycle of *Ten Concert Études* for piano.
18 July: Grażyna's mother dies, following a long and serious illness.

1959

March: premiere in Kraków of *Sonata No. 2* for solo violin, with the composer as soloist.
14 September: at third Warsaw Autumn, premiere of *Music for Stings, Trumpets and Percussion* with WOSPR (Polish National Radio Symphony Orchestra) conducted by Jan Krenz.
November: broadcast of radio opera *The Adventure of King Arthur*.

1960

July: trip to Italy with daughter, Alina; they visit Venice, Rome, Naples, and Capri.
19 September: premier at fourth Warsaw Autumn of *String Quartet No. 6* (first of Grażyna Bacewicz's compositions to be based on the twelve-note system).
Music for Strings, Trumpets and Percussion placed third at UNESCO's International Rostrum of Composers in Paris.
December: elected Vice President of the Polish Composers' Union at its eleventh Annual General Meeting.

1961

21 April: premiere of *Pensieri notturni* at the Venice Biennale.
July: meets brother Vytautas in Paris for the first time in 22 years.

1962

April: trip to USSR. Jury member (for the second time) at the International Tchaikovsky Competition in Moscow.
Visits Leningrad (currently St Petersburg).
17 September: premiere of *Concerto for Large Symphony Orchestra*, at the sixth Warsaw Autumn, played by WOSPR (Polish National Radio Symphony Orchestra) with Witold Rowicki conducting.
Year end: moves to apartment at no. 4 Mochnackiego Street.

1963

30 July: death of husband, Professor Andrzej Biernacki.
29 September: premiere of *Cello Concerto No. 2* at seventh Warsaw Autumn, with National Philharmonic Orchestra, conducted by Witold Krzemieński, with Gaspar Cassadó (for whom the piece was written) as soloist.

1964

24 September: premiere of *Quartet* for four cellos at the eighth Warsaw Autumn, played by Aleksander Ciechański, Jerzy Węsławski, Roman Suchecki, and Marian Raczak.
18 October: premiere of ballet, *Esik in Ostend* at Poznań Opera; libretto by Lech Terpiłowski, after Tadeusz Boy-Żeleński, conducted by Robert Satanowski.
October: trip to Yugoslavia with daughter, Alina; visit takes in Belgrade and Sarajevo.

1965

6 September: premiere in Stockholm of *Musica Sinfonica in Tre Movimenti*, with the National Philharmonic Orchestra and Witold Rowicki conducting.
December: Belgian Government prize and gold medal in the international Queen Elisabeth Competition in Brussels for *Violin Concerto No. 7*.

1966

14 January: premiere of *Violin Concerto No. 7* by Agustín Léon Ara, with the Grand Orchestre Symphonique de la Radiodiffusion-Télévision Belge (Belgian National Broadcasting Symphony Orchestra), conducted by Daniel Sternefeld.
15 May: premiere in Łańcut of *String Quartet No. 7*.
September onwards: teaching composition at State Higher School of Music in Warsaw.

1967

16 July: premiere of *Contradizione* for chamber orchestra at the Summer Festival of Contemporary Music in Hanover (New Hampshire, USA).
Autumn: awarded title of 'Professor'.
November: chair of the jury at the fifth Wieniawski Competition in Poznań.

1968

15 March: premier of *Concerto for Two Pianos* with Jerzy Maksymiuk and Jerzy Witkowski on pianos, and the National Philharmonic Orchestra conducted by Witold Rowicki.

2 October: premiere of *In una parte* at the International Festival of Contemporary Music in Havana with the National Orchestra of Cuba, conducted by Manuel Duchesne Cuzán.

December: travels to Armenia as part of a delegation of Polish composers.

Concerto for Two Pianos is performed in Armenia by Jerzy Maksymiuk and Jerzy Witkowski, with Andrzej Markowski conducting.

1969

15 January: finishes writing her collection of autobiographical short stories, *Znak szczególny* (*A Distinguishing Mark*), which is published the following year (1970).

17 January: following a short illness, Grażyna Bacewicz dies.

Selected Works

For Orchestra

Three Caricatures (1932)
Sinfonietta for string orchestra (1935)
Overture (1943)
Symphony No. 1 (1945)
Symphony No. 2 (1951)
Symphony No. 3 (1952)
Symphony No. 4 (1953)
Concerto for String Orchestra (1948)
Polish Overture (1954)
Music for Strings, Trumpets and Percussion (1958)
Pensieri Notturni (1961)
Musica sinfonica in tre movimenti (1965)
Divertimento for string orchestra (1965)
Contradizione for chamber orchestra (1966)
In una parte (1967)

For solo instrument with orchestra

Violin Concerto No. 1 (1937)
Violin Concerto No. 2 (1945)
Violin Concerto No. 3 (1948)
Violin Concerto No. 4 (1951)
Violin Concerto No. 5 (1954)
Violin Concerto No. 6 (1957)
Violin Concerto No. 7 (1965)
Piano Concerto (1949)

Cello Concerto No. 1 (1951)
Cello Concerto No. 2 (1963)
Concerto for Two Pianos (1966)
Viola Concerto (1968)

Chamber Music

Wind Quintet (1932)
Trio for oboe, violin, and cello (1935)
String Quartet No. 1 (1938)
String Quartet No. 2 (1943)
String Quartet No. 3 (1947)
String Quartet No. 4 (1951)
String Quartet No. 5 (1955)
String Quartet No. 6 (1960)
String Quartet No. 7 (1965)
Sonatas for Violin and Piano
    No. 1 (1945)
    No. 2 (1946)
    No. 3 (1948)
    No. 4 (1949)
    No. 5 (1951)
Quartet for four violins (1949)
Piano Quintet No. 1 (1952)
Piano Quintet No. 2 (1965)
Quartet for four cellos (1963)

For solo violin

Sonata (1941 [unnumbered])
Sonata No. 2 (1958)
Polish Caprice (1949)
Four Caprices (1968)

For piano

Children's Suite (1933)
Piano Sonata No. 1 (1949)
Piano Sonata No. 2 (1953)
Ten Concert Études (1956)
Little Triptych (1965)

For voice

Olympic Cantata for mixed choir and orchestra (1948)
Bell and Chimes, song for voice and piano (1955)
Akropolis, cantata for mixed choir and orchestra (1964)

For stage

Z chłopa król (*The Peasant King*) ballet (1953)
Esik in Ostend comic ballet (1964)
Pożądanie (*Desire*) ballet (1969, unfinished)

Literary works

Znak szczególny (*A Distinguishing Mark*), collection of short stories, Czytelnik (Warsaw, 1970)
Sidła (*Snares*), crime novel, Polskie Wydawnictwo Muzyczne (Kraków, 2018)

References

[1] Maria Modlińska, *Journal*; manuscript in family archives.
[2] Correspondence belonging to the Bacewicz and Biernacki family. Typewritten/word-processed versions exist in the family archives; the original handwritten versions are stored at the Biblioteka Narodowa (National Library) in Warsaw.
[3] Kiejstut Bacewicz, '*Mój brat Witold*' ('My Brother Witold') in *Ruch Muzyczny*, 1986, no. 16.
[4] Grażyna Bacewicz, *Znak szczególny (A Distinguishing Mark)*, Czytelnik (Warsaw, 1970), a collection of short, autobiographical stories.
[5] *Ruch Muzyczny*, 1989, no. 3 (Grażyna Bacewicz interview with Polish Radio's International Service, 1964).
[6] Joanna Sendłak, *With Fire: Grażyna Bacewicz in Love on the Eve of War*, Skarpa (Warsaw, 2018).
[7] Kazimierz Wiłkomirski, *Wspomnienia (Memoir)*, Polskie Wydawnictwo Muzyczne (Kraków, 1971).
[8] Małgorzata Gąsiorowska, *Bacewicz*, Polskie Wydawnictwo Muzyczne (Kraków, 1999); author's interview with Professor Kazimierz Sikorski, 1983; review: Vladas Jakubenas, 'Grażyna Bacewicz Concert', *Rytas*, 1930, no. 86; J.K. interview with Grażyna Bacewicz, *Ruch Muzyczny*, 1947, no. 12; Grażyna Bacewicz's private notes; Włodzimierz Sokorski, *Sztuka w walce o socjalizm* (*Art in the Struggle for Socialism*), 1950; Grażyna Bacewicz's letters to Maria Dziewulska.
[9] Stefan Kisielewski, *Grażyna Bacewicz i jej czasy* (*Grażyna Bacewicz and Her Times*), Polskie Wydawnictwo Muzyczne (Kraków, 1964).
[10] *Grażyna Bacewicz*, a documentary film directed by Ludwik Perski, in collaboration with Zdzisław Sierpiński, Polish Television, 1974. (The same comment by Nadia Boulanger also appears in the film: *Dla ludzi zawsze mam twarz pogodną* (*I always put on a cheerful face [in front of other people]*), screenplay by Małgorzata Gąsiorowska and Dariusz Pawelec, directed by Dariusz Pawelec, Polish Television, 1999.)
[11] Michał Kondracki, 'Serge Prokofiev at a Concert of Contemporary Music', *Nowiny Codzienne* (*The Daily News*), 1936, no. 69.

[12] Joanna Sendłak, *Ostinato – wojenne dni Grażyny Bacewicz* (*Ostinato: The War-Time Days of Grażyna Bacewicz*), Polish Writers' Association, Warsaw Branch, Institute of Literature (Warsaw-Kraków, 2020).
[13] Stefan Kisielewski, *Tygodnik Powszechny*, 9 July 1950 (review).
[14] *Ruch Muzyczny*, 1944, no. 1 (Grażyna Bacewicz's private notes, 1961).
[15] Grażyna Bacewicz, a note in *VIII International Festival of Contemporary Music* (*'Warsaw Autumn'*), Warsaw 1964 (programme notes).
[16] Grażyna Bacewicz, a note in *XI International Festival of Contemporary Music* (*'Warsaw Autumn'*), Warsaw 1967 (programme notes).
[17] Joanna Sendłak, *Vivo – powojenne dni Grażyny Bacewicz* (*The Post-War Days of Grażyna Bacewicz*), unpublished novel.

Further Reading

Bacewicz, Grażyna. *Man and His Work*, material from a ZKP (Polish Composers' Union) session, Polish Composers' Union (Warsaw, 1989).
Gąsiorowska, Małgorzata. *Bacewicz*, Polskie Wydawnictwo Muzyczne (Kraków. 1999).
Kisielewski, Stefan. *Grażyna Bacewicz i jej czasy* (*Grażyna Bacewicz and Her Times*), Polskie Wydawnictwo Muzyczne (Kraków, 1964).
Rosen, Judith. *Grażyna Bacewicz: Her Life and Works*, Friends of Polish Music, University of Southern California (Los Angeles, 1984).
Sendłak, Joanna. *Ostinato – wojenne dni Grażyny Bacewicz* (*Ostinato: The War-Time Days of Grażyna Bacewicz*), Polish Writers' Association, Warsaw Branch, Institute of Literature (Warsaw-Kraków, 2020).
Sendłak, Joanna. *With Fire: Grażyna Bacewicz in Love on the Eve of War*, Skarpa (Warsaw, 2018).
Sendłak, Joanna. *Vivo – powojenne dni Grażyny Bacewicz* (*The Post-War Days of Grażyna Bacewicz*), unpublished novel. https://bacewicz.polmic.pl
Szoka, Marta (ed.). *Grażyna Bacewicz: Konteksty życia i twórczości* (*Grażyna Bacewicz: The Contexts of Her Life and Work*), The Grażyna and Kiejstut Bacewicz Academy of Music in Łódź (Łódź, 2016).
Szoka, Marta (ed.). 'Rodzeństwo Bacewiczów' ('The Bacewicz Siblings'), in *Zeszyt Naukowy* (24), Academy of Music in Łódź (Łódź, 1996).

Index of Names

A
Abendroth, Hermann 79
Absil, Jean 84
Adamska, Zofia 67
Albéniz, Isaac 56
Anosov, Nikolai 85
Ara, Agustín Léon 104, 118
Arct, Michał 44
Astaire, Fred 35
Axer, Erwin 109

B
Bacevičius, Anna née Aliszewska (grandmother) 4
Bacevičius, Petras (Piotr, uncle on father's side) 7, 67
Bacevičius, Piotr (grandfather) 4, 7
Bacevičius, Vincas (father) 1–7, 9, 11–14, 20, 22, 66–7, 113
Bacevičius, Vytautas (Witold/Witek, brother) 3–4, 6–7, 9, 11–14, 18, 20–3, 47–8, 54–5, 58, 64, 88–9, 91, 94, 96–8, 100–2, 104–5, 108–9, 111, 113, 117
Bacewicz (family) 4, 7–17, 36, 38, 42, 45–6, 88–9, 113
Bacewicz, Kiejstut (Kiej, Tutik, brother) 6–7, 9–14, 16–18, 21–3, 31, 32, 37–9, 46–53, 56, 60, 61, 66–7, 72, 77–81, 88–9, 91, 96–7, 102, 107, 110–11, 115, 116
Bacewicz, Wanda (Wan, Wandzia, sister) 6, 8–9, 12–13, 17, 20, 24, 28–32, 37, 41–2, 44, 46–52, 66–7, 73–6, 79–81, 85, 89, 94–95, 97, 102, 104–5, 107, 109–11
Bach, Johann Sebastian 24, 44, 54, 57, 64, 68, 72, 75, 81
Baird, Tadeusz 60, 73, 76, 78, 80, 110
Baranowicz-Bacewicz, Halina (Halszka, sister-in-law) 14, 17–18, 21, 46, 48–9, 51, 72, 81, 88, 96, 107
Barcewicz, Stanisław 76
Bartók, Béla 33, 81, 89–90
Bąkowski, Stanisław 101
Beethoven, Ludwig van 11, 44, 72
Bellini, Vincenzo 11
Berg, Alban 89, 90
Bezverkhny, Mikhail 107
Bibrowski, Mieczysław 108, 109
Biel, Stanisław 86, 87
Bierdiajew, Walerian 74, 116
Biernacka, Alina (Alinka, daughter; married name: Sendłak) 30, 40, 44–7, 49, 51, 65, 67–8, 71, 72, 73, 74–5, 79, 84, 92, 94–6, 102, 105, 114, 117
Biernacka-Ciccotti, Jadwiga (sister-in-law) 92
Biernacki, Andrzej (husband) 25–6, 28–33, 35, 37–8, 41, 44–5, 47–51, 53, 56, 58, 72, 74, 79, 83–6, 88–9, 92, 96–8, 110, 114, 118
Biernacki (family) 30–1, 35, 42, 49–50
Biernacki, Mieczysław (Miecio) Kwiryn (brother-in-law) 30, 31

INDEX OF NAMES

Bierut, Bolesław 83, 84
Bleuzet, Louis 34
Boccaccio, Giovanni 94
Bogucka, Janina 41
Bogucki, Andrzej 41
Bonaventura, Mario di 106
Bosch, Hieronymus 42
Bouchoné (impresario) 53
Boulanger, Lili 54, 101
Boulanger, Nadia 22, 33, 82, 84–5, 101, 114
Boy-Żeleński, Tadeusz 101, 118
Brahms, Johannes 65, 81, 91

C
Calvet, Joseph 71
Cassadó, Gaspar 98, 100, 118
Chomiński, Józef 60, 69
Chopin, Fryderyk 11, 39, 49, 56, 60, 72, 76, 115
Ciechański, Aleksander 118
Comte-Wilgocka, Adela 17
Cuzán, Manuel Duchesne 106, 119
Cwojdziński, Andrzej 80
Czajkowski, Renard 109
Czartoryski (family) 3
Czyż, Henryk 106

D
Danczowska, Kaja 107
Dąmbski (family) 3
Detoni, Dubravko 105
Dimov, Dimo 105
Dobkiewicz, Antoni 15, 51, 113
Dobrowolski, Andrzej 76, 78
Dohnányi, Ernst von 54, 56
Dołżycki, Adam 39
Dorys, Benedykt 56
Drewniakówna, Maria 77–8
Drzewiecki, Conrad 101
Dubiska, Irena 43, 50, 88, 107, 114, 117
Dukas, Paul 26
Dworzaczek, Aloyzy 5
Dzierżanowski, Feliks 12
Dziewoński, Edward 108
Dziewulska, Maria 75, 80, 91

E
Ekier (family) 48, 67

Ekier, Jan 58
Elzenberg, Henryk 18
Elisabeth, Queen of Belgium 76, 104, 118

F
Falla, Manuel de 54
Feicht, Hieronim 78
Fellini, Federico 92
Fischer, Ludwig 41
Fiszer, Edward 91
Fitelberg, Grzegorz ('Ficio') 21, 23, 26, 30, 57, 61, 65, 69, 71, 72, 86, 114, 115
Fitelberg, Jerzy 32
Flesch, Carl 24, 114
Fournier, Jean 107

G
Gadomski, Henryk 72
Gagnebin, Henri 107
Gałczyński, Konstanty Ildefons 72
Gargi, Balvant 83
Gauguin, Paul 95
Georgescu, George 95
Germain, Jean 54, 115
Gertler, André 88
Gimpel, Bronisław 87
Godard, Benjamin 11
Gomułka, Władysław 84–5
Göring, Hermann 31, 46
Górecki, Henryk Mikołaj 109
Górzyński, Zdzisław 51, 58
Gradstein, Alfred 65
Grieg, Edvard 20
Grigaitiene, Władysława 21
Grohman, Henryk 1
Groński, Stanisław 86
Grudzieński, Antoni 6
Guillou, Jean 105
Guiron, M. 87

H
Halber, Roman 29
Handel, George Frideric 20, 57
Hanicki (brothers) 5, 6
Hennertowa, Jadwiga 23
Henry, Harold J. 11
Herbst, Edward 6, 9
Herbst, Matylda (née Scheibler) 6

Hess, Rudolf 31
Hessen vel Goetzen, Kazimierz 5
Hindemith, Paul 29, 33
Hitler, Adolf 31–3, 38
Holeček, Alfred 61
Hösl, Albert 40
Hurst, George 106

I
Iwanow, Igor 104
Iwaszkiewicz, Jarosław 57

J
Jahnke, Zdzisław 68
Janowski, Piotr 107
Jarzębski, Józef 18, 21, 44, 68, 76
Jasiński, Andrzej 88

K
Kačinskas, Jeronimas 21
Kadosa, Pál 84
Kamasa, Stefan 104, 106, 107
Kamiliarov, Emil 107
Karłowicz, Mieczysław 52
Kasprowicz, Jan 32
Kazuro, Stanisław 19
Kątski, Antoni (*see* Kontski)
Khrushchev, Nikita 84
Kiesewetter, Tomasz 54, 115
Kijeńska-Dobkiewiczowa, Helena 5, 10, 12, 14, 15, 113
Kisielewski, Stefan 21, 32, 57, 79, 80, 93, 95, 108, 112
Klecki, Paul (*see* Kletzki)
Kletzki, Paul 54, 115
Kmitowa, Lidia 29
Kobuszewski, Jan 108
Kogan, Leonid 95
Kondracki, Michał 29
Kontski, (Kątski) Anton de 11
Korwin-Kossakowska, Antonina 5
Korwin-Szymanowska, Stanisława 31
Kotoński, Włodzimierz 76
König, Christoph 87
Krenz, Jan 73, 80, 86, 90, 91, 117
Kruczkowski, Leon 61
Krzemieński, Witold 64, 70, 100, 118
Kulka, Konstanty Andrzej 107

Kuryluk, Karol 53

L
Lachowska, Stefania 80
Lang, Walter 35
Lardelli, Jan Jakub 39
Lechoń, Jan 34
Lefeld, Jerzy 24
Leo XIII (Pope) 3
Leszetycki, Teodor 15
Lewicki, Czesław 32
Lilpop, Edward 10
Lissa, Zofia 59, 60, 65
Lutowsławski, Witold 24, 41, 46, 58, 60, 65, 67, 72, 73, 84, 85, 90
Lutosławskis (Mr and Mrs) 65, 73, 85, 101

Ł
Łabuński, Feliks Roderyk 23
Łosakiewicz, Bohdan 26, 33
Łosakiewicz, Maria (Marysia) 81
Łosakiewicz, Wanda 32
Łosakiewiczes (Mr and Mrs) 78
Łukasiewicz, Jan 18

M
Madey, Bogusław 111
Majer, Józef 5
Maklakiewicz, Jan 13
Maksymiuk, Jerzy 108, 109, 119
Malawski, Artur 60
Maréchal, Maurice 95
Marek, Tadeusz 19
Markowski, Andrzej 93, 101, 106, 109, 119
Martinon, Jean 85
Matisse, Henri 95
Medtner, Nikolai 16
Mendelssohn, Felix 16, 54
Menuhin, Yehudi 88, 117
Michałowski, Aleksander (bass) 44
Michałowski, Aleksander (pianist) 1, 2
Mickiewicz, Adam 79, 108
Mierzejewski, Mieczysław 52, 115
Miszczyk, Stanisław 73, 74
Modlińska, Aniela (aunt) 2, 3
Modlińska, Maria (mother; married name: Bacewiczowa) 1–14, 17, 20, 46, 62–70, 72–89, 113

Modliński (family) 3
Modliński, Józef (great-uncle) 3
Modliński, Stanisław (grandfather) 3
Morawski, Eugeniusz 19
Mozart, Wolfgang Amadeus 11, 12, 55
Mussorgsky, Modest 54
Mycielski, Zygmunt 59, 65, 85

N
Nadgryzowski, Sergiusz 71
Nehru, Jawaharlal 83
Neuhaus, Harry 95
Nizioł, Bartłomiej 87
Noskowski, Zygmunt 2, 5

O
Ochlewski, Tadeusz 42, 52, 53
Oistrakh, David 84, 88, 95, 117
Oistrakh, Igor 68, 71
Orkisz, Andrzej 104

P
Padlewski, Roman 39
Paganini, Niccolò 54
Palester, Roman 19, 32
Palesters (Mr and Mrs) 51
Panufnik, Andrzej 19, 32, 46, 60, 67, 70, 78
Panufniks (Mr and Mrs) 65
Parrenin, Jacques 85, 92
Perkowski, Piotr 41, 79
Persinger, Louis 88
Pessard, Émile 11
Piatigorsky, Gregor 95
Picasso, Pablo 95, 108
Pichon, Monique 62
Pindar 56
Plato 90
Ponikowski (Mr) 75
Poulenc, Francis 54
Principe, Remy 107
Prokofiev, Sergei 16, 29, 81
Pryssewiczówna, Janina 12, 16, 17, 113
Przyboś, Julian 53
Pugnani, Gaetano 54

R
Rachoń, Stefan 91
Raczak, Marian 118
Raczkowski, Władysław 51
Radziwiłł (family) 3
Raja, Krishna 83
Ravel, Maurice 54, 81
Raybould, Clarence 56
Rembrandt, Harmenszoon van Rijn 95
Rogers, Ginger 35
Rosenthal, Moriz 1
Rostafińskis (Mr and Mrs) 78
Roussel, Albert 33
Rowicki, Witold 61, 76, 95, 100, 103, 107, 108, 116, 118, 119
Rowickis (Mr and Mrs) 65, 102
Rubinstein, Arthur 72, 76
Rudnicki, Edmund 38–41, 47, 67, 85
Rudnickis (Mr and Mrs) 74, 77, 78
Rudziński, Witold 32, 78, 80
Rytel, Piotr 19

S
Sádlo, Karel Pravoslav 95
Sádlo, Miloš 64
Salviati, Antonio 10
Satanowski, Robert 101, 118
Scheibler, Karol 6, 9, 11
Schmitt, Florent 34
Schönberg, Arnold 89, 90
Seiter, William A. 35
Sendłak, Jerzy (son-in-law) 96, 102
Sendłak, Joanna (granddaughter) 65, 105–6, 110
Serocki, Kazimierz 70, 76, 78
Serockis (Mr and Mrs) 73
Shkolnikova, Nelli 71
Shostakovich, Dmitri 95
Sikorski, Kazimierz 14, 16, 18, 19, 21, 23, 51, 55, 56, 65, 73, 76, 78, 79, 81, 83, 84, 92
Sikorski, Tomasz 80
Skowron, Lidia 80
Skrowaczewski, Stanisław 80
Sławoj Składkowski, Felicjan 37
Słowacki, Juliusz 40
Smendzianka, Regina 85, 86, 103, 117
Sokorski, Włodzimierz 59, 72
Spiess, Ludwik 3
Spisak, Andrée 101, 102
Spisak, Michał 32, 101, 102

Stalin, Joseph 59–60, 69, 84
Stanisław August (Poniatowski, King of Poland) 3
Starzyński, Stefan 35, 36, 38
Sternefeld, Daniel 104, 118
Stockhausen, Karlheinz 89
Strauss, Richard 31
Stravinsky, Igor 54, 101, 102
Suchecki, Roman 118
Sulikowski, Jerzy 23
Swinarski, Artur Maria 74
Sygietyński, Tadeusz 51
Szałowski, Antoni 19, 32, 54
Szamotulska, Jadwiga 79
Szczepańskis (Mr and Mrs) 78
Szeligowski, Tadeusz 65
Szeryng, Henryk 72, 107
Szigeti, Joseph 95
Szpilman, Władysław 41, 87, 104
Szpinalski, Stanisław 60
Sztompka, Henryk 71
Szymanowski, Karol 15, 19, 20, 22, 39, 46, 54
Szymonowicz, Zbigniew 77

Ś
Śledziński, Stefan 57, 115
Śliwiński, Józef 1
Śmigły-Rydz, Edward 35
Śnieckowski, Seweryn 29

T
Tagore, Rabindranath 32
Tatarkiewicz, Władysław 18
Tawroszewicz, Jan 104
Temple, Shirley 35
Terpiłowski, Lech 101, 118
Teutsch, Karol 103
Tintoretto, Jacopo 92
Tippett, Michael 84
Tomaszewski, Antoni 6
Touret, André 22, 114
Trzonek, Henryk 39, 42, 45
Turczyński, Józef 18
Turski, Zbigniew 56, 63, 88
Tuwim, Julian 72, 130

U
Umeda, Ryōchū 18
Umińska, Eugenia (Genia) 39–43, 46, 51, 79, 88, 107, 114, 117

V
Veronese, Paolo 92
Vito de, Gioconda 71
Vivaldi, Antonio 51

W
Waljewski, Szymon 13
Wamlek, Hans 77
Wąsik, Wiktor 18
Webern, Anton 89, 90
Węsławski, Jerzy 118
Widulińska, Zofia 85
Wiechowicz, Stanisław 79
Wieczorkowska (Mrs) 2
Wieniawski, Henryk 24, 54, 56
Wiesenberg, Feliks 12
Wiłkomirska, Irena 51
Wiłkomirska, Maria 39
Wiłkomirska, Wanda 76, 77, 79, 116
Wiłkomirski, Kazimiez 16, 39, 43, 51, 98
Wiśniewski, Stefan 46
Witas, Jerzy 54
Witkowski, Jerzy 108, 109, 119
Witwicki, Władysław 18
Wodiczko, Bohdan 65, 69, 73, 116
Woytowicz, Bolesław 39, 42, 43, 46
Wroński, Tadeusz 77, 107

Z
Zatorski (Mr) 75
Zdzitowiecka, Natalia Anna (grandmother; married name: Modlińska) 2, 3, 12
Zdzitowiecki, Władysław (great-uncle) 3
Zimbalist, Efrem 95
Zimmer, Aleksander 2, 5

Ż
Żuławski, Wawrzyniec 40, 61, 65, 67, 79, 86–7
Żuławskis (family) 87